ESCAPE TO PELICAN LAKE

A book of poetry, lyrics, and short stories

WILL REUHL

Copyright @ 2022 by Will Reuhl

Escape to Pelican Lake

All rights reserved.

No part of this publication may be reproduced or transmitted
In any form or by any means electronic or mechanical, including photocopy,
Recording, or any information storage and retrieval system now known or invented,
Without permission in writing from the publisher, except by a reviewer
Who wishes to quote brief passages in connection with a review written
For inclusion in a magazine, newspaper, or broadcast.

Print ISBN: 978-1-66788-340-3
Ebook ISBN: 978-1-66788-341-0

Printed in the United States of America

Dedication

To the young child in all of us.
Never stop dreaming,
Never stop loving,
Never stop making friends!
These are three items
You can never have too much of...

"A Winner Is a Dreamer Who Never Gives Up."

—Nelson Mandela

Table of Contents

(A Brief) INTRODUCTION	1
A Day at the Lake	5
A Minnie Life	7
All my Heart	9
Always Kiss Me Goodnight	13
An American Voyage	15
Baby Girl	17
Being a Reuhl (Rule Number One)	22
Billionaire	25
7-10 Split	29
Catch Me When I Fall	31
Caught in the Rain	33
Chance of a Lifetime	35
Classic Cliches	39
Do Not Look Now	41
Emily in Paris	43
For the First Time	45
Freedom	47
Hard to Understand	49
Have a Little Fun	51
Hit the Door	53
HOLD ON TO ME	55
Home Sweet Home (Alabama)-	57
Into the Night	59
Last Dance	61
Last Forever More	63
LONE STAR	65
Love Letter	67
Love Letter Reply	71
Love Struck	79
Me and Tucker	81
Moving Up or Moving Out	83

My Little Butterfly	87
My Old Yellow Jeep	89
Next Jen	91
No Flowers, No Rain	93
No Way Out	95
One Latte'	97
One Lens, One Picture, One Time	99
Pelican Port Resort	101
Perfect Day	107
Random Rhymes	109
Ready, Aim, Higher	111
RIDGEWOOD WAY	113
Rocky Mountain High	117
Rollercoaster Ride	119
Running Water	121
Seattle Nights	123
Singapore Sings	127
Sit For a While	131
Summertime	137
SUMMER	139
THAT IS ALL I KNOW (so far)	141
The Right Way	143
The Rules of Golf	145
The Significance of Twelve (12)	147
Three Seconds (in a lifetime…)	151
Together Forever?	153
Too Much	155
UP	157
Walk on the Beach	159
Warm Hugs	161
Where Eagles Soar	163
Where the Wildflowers Grow	165
Words from Confusion	167
Words of Wisdom	169
You Come as You Are	171

(A Brief) INTRODUCTION

In book two, I tried capturing more fun. More joy, more laughter, more Love…

Scholars would examine my books and wonder why I spell through as "thru?"

A lot has to do with the rhythm of the rhyme and my personality. I also add …

At the end of many of my poems to give them an extended meaning.

Using … means that there is more to come. More life, more activities, more Fun.

I was fortunate growing up to spend a lot of time on Big Pelican Lake in Northern Minnesota!

My summers were carefree and full of life. I was constantly, surrounded by friends and family.

We had many good times at the Lake. That is why I titled this book-Escape to Pelican Lake!

Again, this book is rather random, just like life! I do this to be unpredictable and add a little spice.

I now observe the world more as a poet, hearing rhyme everywhere I go. Be careful of what you say because it could become the subject of my poetry.

I have always had an ear for music and been in love with love from an early age.

Life is music! It sets the tone, and fills you with memories when you are all alone. It greets you like a friend visiting your home. I cannot think how boring life would be without music! How would we express ourselves? How would we comfort ourselves? How would "we get to where we are getting to?" Just ask Rascal Flatts to sing a note or two! Music fills our lives…

Once again, I need to thank my family for putting up with my writing shenanigans! Without your support, none of this is possible!

I have always been a doodler and write everything down. There is music and poetry consistently playing in my head. For some this can be exhausting, but for me, I find it exhilarating. I am so happy to share this with you! I hope you can relate with a thought or two...

I do not write or sing for myself but to make others happier and joyful. There is far too much destruction in the world. We need to spread positive thoughts and ideas! A smile and kind word does not cost you anything. You need to give more away. Spread the word today!

I lose my voice once a year to laryngitis, which helps me reflect on how vital speech is.

I recognize words have meaning and consequences on how they, and we- are perceived.

I once heard it said that yesterday is in the past, tomorrow is an unknown, and today is but a song.

Today is a gift - that is why we call it the Present! Enjoy every day, especially - TODAY...

Photo by Joshua Earle on Unsplash.com

Photo by Michael T. Rose on Unsplash.com

A Day at the Lake

I am most comfortable sitting down at the lake,
Feeling the wind blow in my face,
Listening to leaves rustle and the trees sway.
Birds chirping and the fish jumping out with a splash,
I look up at the sky and see the sun,
It is about one and time to have some fun.
Should I jump in the lake and cool down,
Should I run and get my fishing pole or catch some sun?
My wish is to be one with nature and not miss a beat,
I waited too long and now Leena has taken my seat.
It does not matter much to me as long as I am at the Lake,
Maybe I will sit under this tree and write for a while,
Have a dance party with my granddaughter, I said with a smile.
The skies become darker as a summer storm blows in,
We can see the streak of rain come across the lake,
We grab our towels, head to the cabin, and make our escape.
Rain and wind create nature's perfect sound machine,
Projecting white noise to put you in a deep sleep.
A bird crows outside like the sound of a strobe light in a dark room,
Warning us to get inside before the storm hits us from all sides.
Once in the cabin, all we hear is the clock on the wall. Tic, toc, tic, toc, tic.
Natural light goes away by darkness as the storm blows by.
Trees encircle and protect us from the heart of this disruption.
It blows thru like a locomotive blowing its horn on the railroad track.
It reminds us how lucky we are to have each other and takes us back.
Peace and serenity now fill the air- as a light breeze blows my hair.
Mother Nature has a way of balancing the sun, wind, and rain;
she knows when it is time to do it Again and Again.

Photo by Anjuli on Unsplash.com

A Minnie Life

What is that thing I like to do,
Look my grandparents put down some food!
It would be very nice to drink water with that,
To run up and down the hallway till I get your hat!
Oops, I drank too much water and have to pee,
Please take me out, so I can go on my favorite tree!
Wait, are those people walking down the street?
I am so excited to say hi without a peep.
I love my family,
I love my bone,
I am lucky to call this my home.
Wait a minute, wait a minute - you are sitting in my spot,
I will climb on you and the couch, whether you move.
Please take me to the park or for a ride,
I am so excited; - some say -, I have a beautiful mind.
Do not hold back; keep me on the leash - that's fine,
Just make sure I get to see Milo, - from time to time.
Milo is my best friend and my brother,
We look nothing alike because we have different Mothers.
I am the luckiest dog on Earth,
Because I was Leena's Christmas present, - right after my birth.

Photo by Brittney Burnett on Unsplash.com

"Your work is to discover
your world
And then with all
your heart
Give yourself to it."
–Buddha

All my Heart

All my heart I give to you my darling,
All my heart I give to you.
Yesterday, today, and tomorrow,
What was and should be.
In my arms or not,
You are always in my heart!

I never walk alone in the dark,
I never walk alone in the park.
I never show how much I care,
I never say no to you my darling.
I never come home without a smile,
I never walk without you in my mind.

All my heart I give to you my darling,
All my heart I give to you.
Yesterday, today, and tomorrow,
What was and should be.
In my arms or not,
You are always in my heart!

It never seems that you hear my remarks,
It never stops me from knowing you are smart.

It never crosses my mind when you are not there,
It never seems to be entirely fair.
It never rings when you are not there,
It never even opens or tears.

All my heart I give to you my darling,
All my heart I give to you.
Yesterday, today, and tomorrow,
What was and should be.
In my arms or not,
You are always in my heart!

We never follow anyone else's rules when we start,
We never stop to notice when it comes to matters of the heart.
We never want this feeling to end though rare,
We never cry out or say it is not fair.
We smile and go bye and sometimes stare,
It is those rare moments, in life, that we cannot despair.

All my heart I give to you my darling,
All my heart I give to you.
Yesterday, today, and tomorrow,
What was and should be.
In my arms or not,
You are always in my heart!

"You'll never be criticized by someone who is **doing more than you.** You'll always be criticized by **someone doing less.** Rember that."
– Denzel Washington

Photo by Sabina Tone on Unsplash.com

Always Kiss Me Goodnight

When it is time to go to sleep at night,
When you hear a strange sound and take flight,
Always kiss me goodnight.
No matter how tough you had it all day,
Remember it is important to thank God for the day,
And always kiss me goodnight.
Turn off the television it is very late,
We need to sort out our priorities, not leave them to fate,
And always kiss me goodnight.
You kissed me in the rays of the moonlight,
It was a harvest moon in plain sight,
And you always kissed me goodnight!
Lest we forget to embrace,
Lest we not concentrate,
Always kiss me goodnight.
Whether it is too cold or too hot,
Whether you do not feel like it or want to stop,
Always kiss me goodnight.
I know it is late, I know you are worried,
Even if your plans do not include me,
Always kiss me goodnight.
Here we are, lying in the same bed at night,
Worried about what the next day will bring without flight,
But Always kiss me goodnight.
This year has now come and gone,
Like a song we want to sing along,
And Always kiss me goodnight.

Photo by Andres Dallimonti on Unsplash.com

An American Voyage

We came to America by ship,
It was a long voyage with rough waters and sailors getting seasick.
If it was not for those rum barrels, I am not sure we would have made it!
We had plenty of food and the crew was happy at first,
Until the sea opened like a whale's mouth, eating fish and quenching its thirst.
Once close to land, the birds would appear,
Like an angel in the night, they would disappear.
Navigating the seas at night was not an easy task,
Stars guided us across the vast body of water with a sturdy mast.
Do not get the wrong idea, but this captains best companion was his flask.
A rough day at sea meant we would most often have a calm night,
Some sailors at the port would have enough and take flight.
Each port offered a different view,
With plenty of sailors to fill in as our new crew.
Days went by as the weeks went on,
We enjoyed the journey with an occasional song.
Besides the storms or the rough seas,
We worried about pirates, maybe two or three...
Was I worried, or was this the siren of the sea?
At that moment, I knew our destination was not far,
Days would turn into weeks; at night, there was a show of stars.
Landing on Plymouth Rock that morn there was fog and clouds,
All we had were the clothes on our backs and our shrouds.
As soon as we heard "Land ho,"- the crew let out a good cheer,
We would make camp and forage for a year.
That was the greatest journey of my life,
We made great strides, a new beginning, thru all the strife.

Photo by Kelly Sikkema on Unsplah.com

"The older I get,
The greater power I seem
to have To help the world".
- Susan B. Anthony

Baby Girl

You are the girl that I want,
You are the Girl I am not,
You are that girl, oh so hot!
You are up all night,
You are out of sight,
You make me hold back my delight.

There are moonbeams in your hair,
There is laughter in the air.
Your eyes are like sapphires in the night,
A light shining bright, saying it will be all right!
I want to spend it with you - The rest of my life.

You are the girl that I want,
You are the Girl I am not,
You are that girl, oh so hot!
You are up all night,
You are out of sight,
You make me hold back my delight.

Sit down for a while and chat,
I never said that we would do that.
Maybe just set a spell and forget for a while,
I said to myself until I looked at her with a smile.

Did I really say that out - loud?
Did you really want to make me proud?
I am so in Love with you; I don't know what to do.

You are the girl that I want,
You are the Girl I am not,
You are that girl, oh so hot!
You are up all night,
You are out of sight,
You make me hold back my delight.

Just look outside for a big surprise,
Just hunt for that Easter basket in the light of day,
You, so mesmerize me with those beautiful eyes.
Just sit right down, and you will realize,
There is more to life than suspicion and wealth,
You are so adorable to me. Just wait, and you will see.
Life's consequence, it all comes for free…

You are the girl that I want,
You are the Girl I am not,
You are that girl, oh so hot!
You are up all night,
You are out of sight,
You make me hold back my delight.

Anybody with artistic ambitions is always trying to reconnect with the way they saw things as a child.

-Tim Burton

Photo by Brett Jordan on Unsplash.com

"What is happiness except the simple harmony between a man and the life he leads?"
– Albert Camus

Being a Reuhl
(Rule Number One)

William George Reuhl-first name from father and middle name from great grandfather.

Son of a meat packer and a homemaker. The fifth child of six children in a German-American, middle- class, suburban family.

My father was large and in charge, loud and proud. My mother was petite but strong, gentle and kind.

Together they raised six children who would blow your mind...

My father would tell us, "Do it right the first time or don't do it at all".

My father never met a meal he did not love- "the Best he ever had".

My mother was the love of his life, the domesticator, the peacemaker.

She was the balance, the reinforcer, and the comfort to us all.

Two of my mother's favorite sayings were "to forgive and forget" and "Beauty is in the eyes of the beholder."

My daily montra is: "Do your best, and hopefully your best is good enough."

We were taught to smile, and the whole world would smile back! As I grew up, I found that smiling did not always return a smile, but it never hurt to try (smiles are free).

My parents were not perfect, but they tried hard, raised us to be kind, and did what they thought was Right. We appreciated the great effort and energy it took.

"Gratitude and attitude are not challenges, they are choices." – Robert Braathe

"Feeling gratitude and not expressing it is like wrapping a present and not giving it." – William Arthur Ward

The Reuhl family is a troop of optimistic teasers, over achievers, and fortunate pleasers.

We love to drink; we, love to think; - we love to laugh; we love to eat; we love to treat. - Yes, we love to treat you to a song and a dance. - We love

- love, and love having loving thoughts. My mother always said, "You are a lover not a fighter."

Some of us like to ride, some of us like to swim, but All of us like to win...

Music sets the mood, lights the fire, and crests the moon. We all love music.

Many of us love a song until dawn, and some like to sing along.

Thanks, Mom for the music! Thanks Dad for the rhythm! Thank God for both!

The days and nights would have been lonely without your constant love and ambition,

You reinforced it every day and showed us many family traditions.

My children and grandchildren will understand what it is to be a Reuhl by understanding the past and following all the rules. I made some of the rules, I know all the rules, but most importantly, I am proud to be a Reuhl!

Photo by Nate Johnston on Unsplash.com

Billionaire

If I were a billionaire,
I could wear diamonds in my hair.
Riding down the boulevard in my blue Belaire,
Sticking my head out the window with the wind in my hair.
My imagination would be free to live anywhere,
My goodwill and charity would be spread everywhere.
If I were a billionaire…

I would climb the highest mountain,
Swim the deepest ocean - just to spend one moment with you.
We could travel the world together,
Not worry about the weather - as long as – we're together.
We walk hand and hand,
Just you and me, my friend.

If I were a billionaire,
I could wear diamonds in my hair.
Riding down the boulevard in my blue Belaire,
Sticking my head out the window with the wind in my hair.
My imagination would be free to live anywhere,
My goodwill and charity would be spread everywhere.
If I were a billionaire…

We would laugh, smile, and sit for awhile,
Walk and talk with me, while we sail down the Nile.

Each day will be special,
Living our whole life for the world to see,

Nothing would ever get in the way of you and me.
Whether walking down the boulevard,
Or strolling down the Champs-Elysees in gay Paris.
It will be so much fun for you and me.

If I were a billionaire,
I could wear diamonds in my hair.
Riding down the boulevard in my blue Belaire,
Sticking my head out the window with the wind in my hair.
My imagination would be free to live anywhere,
My goodwill and charity would be spread everywhere.
If I were a billionaire…

Just you and me in an African tree,
On an exotic safari down under, feeling wild and free.
Walking across the Great Wall of China,
Or scaling a castle wall in a jolly old English countryside.
Let's go down to Carolina, where nothing could be finer.
Imagine it now, and you could be there,
Maybe flying in my lear jet thru the air with a great big stare.

If I were a billionaire,
I could wear diamonds in my hair.
Riding down the boulevard in my blue Belaire,
Sticking my head out the window with the wind in my hair.
My imagination would be free to live anywhere,
My goodwill and charity would be spread everywhere.
If I were a billionaire…

Istock Photo on Unsplash.com

Photo by Dalton Smith on Unsplash.com

7-10 Split

We clowned around in a town nearby-We passed hell, along the way, but I could not tell.

We drank wine and had a good time, as time went by.

We glanced out, and saw a hill - but could not stand alone.

We had no sense of control, now here to go,

We had arrived, but we did not know where to go.

We did not know where we were, how we had gotten so far,

We had to turn around or needed to push the car.

We landed in a place called Amusement Alley,

We were not amused, not even Allie.

We saw images of light illuminating a wall,

We sensed it all with the roll of a ball.

We got off a strike with no time to spare,

We saw it was ready to strike Midnight, but we did not care.

We realized it was three hundred times harder to get back,

We could not turn it around because the pins were stacked.

We had to relax and find our way back before the other team attacked.

We had to reach a perfect game; an, achievement very few could do,

We had to knock them down before we were thru.

We could mansplain our way thru to find an end to a means, a rip in our jeans.

We were not running out of time but did not know if this was our time.

We knew Scott, who knew the spot and could help us thru this time.

We felt the end of our lane, after hopping a train at the end of the tracks.

We saw no footprints in our bowling shoes, just an impression in our mind.

We needed to visualize our stride to get where we were going that night,

We needed to concentrate and keep our eyes on the prize,

We knew we were close, I surmised, but we must not take flight.

We would keep our feet on the ground, rinse and repeat, and rise above any defeat.

Photo by Stephan Walker on Unsplash.com

> "I learned that courage was not the absence of fear, But the triumph over it."
> —Nelson Mandela

Catch Me When I Fall

I am watching you watching me,
I like all that I can see.
From the corner of my eye I can see,
From the corner of your mind, are you watching me?
All the pictures, all the time,
I am glancing at the photos in my mind.
You may never see it again or find that special friend,
Someone who cares and is so kind until the end.
Nothing ever lasts forever; that, is why you are so special.
I see my reflection in the mirror on the wall,
You see your reflection everyday by the waterfall.
One moment of time has passed,
One memory known to last.
Take a picture again, so you lest not forget,
It is by and by throughout the looking glass.
I fell into the rabbit hole,
All I wanted to do was save your soul.
Another breath of silence is in the air,
Should I not pass this way or lest I dare?
Hush is but a pause from breath to breath,
Lust is but a sign from caress to caress.
I must leave you but only for a short while,
Do not think less of me-just cherish that smile.

Photo by Cristophe Dutour on Unsplash.com

"The way I see it,
If you want the rainbow,
You gotta put up with
the rain."
-Dolly Parton

Caught in the Rain

Let the trees stop the rain,
I will play on thru the pain.
If I master it, it will be my gain!
Hold on for your part, hold onto the reins, hold onto your heart.
This is a good walk ruined; this, is a stretch and a mood written.
Maybe I should hit with strength; maybe, I should hit for length.
If you drive for show and putt for dough,
Why can't you stay out all day and play twice in a row?
The wind blows the trees and acts up all the bees.
Be aggressive, go for it all,
Tomorrow is not promised to us all.
Keep your head down and swing thru,
These are life lessons that apply to golf too.
So hit the ball thru the trees, hit it against a strong breeze,
Hit it straight without an iron, use your woods to please.
I'm not sure what is more fun for you or me.
I know a hole - in - one would be the ultimate fun,
Or, as my mother said, a hole in two is not bad for you.
So take your seven wood and hit it good,
High, up in the sky, up into the heavens, I knew you could!
Maybe you should unleash the hounds or add a little swing oil?
No matter what comes or may it may not create a boil.
Stay calm. This is a game for gentlemen; let us play,
There is no reason to yell, or throw anything, especially today.
Whether it is an eagle, a birdie, or a par, no matter what you are,
You better have a witness or they may not believe it went that far.
A weekend warrior, an amateur, a rising star; this is your game, your time, your fame.

Photo by Arturo Rey on Unsplash.com

Chance of a Lifetime

God holds out his hand to give you one chance.

So grab hold of someone you love; you, are special - a gift from above.

If given only one chance, would you take it? Or just give it a glance.

A spiritual choice in a lifetime, In a lifetime of chances...

Do not be confused by outside distractions; listen, to your heart thru all infractions.

No one is without fault in the eyes of the Lord; He, told us to listen and put down our swords.

The storm that was sent to break you, Will be the storm that God uses to make you.

He will pick you up when you fall; He, will never let you go...

God holds out his hand to give you one chance.

So grab hold of someone you love; you, are so special - a gift from above.

If given only one chance, would you take it? Or just give it a glance.

A spiritual choice in a lifetime, In a lifetime of chances...

The Lord is my shepherd. Nothing shall I want. He takes me to the highest mountain; he,

makes me swim thru stormy seas.

He is my Savior. When he looks at me, I see that which he wants me to see,

He shows me all the possibilities.

Once I was blind but now I see, Once I was deaf but now I hear, If I will follow there is nothing

to fear...

God holds out his hand to give you one chance.

So grab hold of someone you love, You are so special - a gift from above.

If given only one chance, would you take it? Or just give it a glance.

A spiritual choice in a lifetime, In a lifetime of chances...

You must hold on to hope and love, Every day is a gift, a kind of present.

Live in the present, but remember the past, God has a plan for you- a future that will last.

It shall last an eternity for all of mankind, Just remember to try your best to be kind.

My father always said to do it right the first time, Or do not do it at all.

For you only live once, But if you do it right- Once is Enough!

God holds out his hand to give you one chance.

So grab hold of someone you love, You are so special - a gift from above.

If given only one chance, would you take it? Or just give it a glance.

A spiritual choice in a lifetime, In a lifetime of chances...

AMEN

Photo by Clark Vanderbeken on Unsplash.com

"PLEASE WATCH OUT
FOR EACH OTHER AND
LOVE AND
FORGIVE EVERYBODY.
IT'S A GOOD LIFE,
ENJOY IT."
-JIM HENSON

Photo by Paulina Milde on Unsplash.com

Classic Cliches

Don't cry because it is over, smile because it happened.
If it ain't broke, don't fix it.
A penney saved is a penny earned.
A bird in the hand is worth two in the bush.
Jack of all trades, master of none.
That is water under the bridge.
Every cloud has a silver lining.
When pigs fly…
It's raining cats and dogs.
Don't bite the hand that feeds you.

These are words originally, I did not say,
These are words that won't go away.
These things are still said today,
These are things stuck in every head.
We quote others without regard or meaning,
We judge upon a report card and begin dreaming…

Photo by Hayley Murray on Unsplash.com

Do Not Look Now

Looking down on the ground,
Looking all around.
Here and there, but everywhere.
I can see you now,
I can see you inside and out.
I can see you, for who you are,
Time and time again.
Then we go back to a life well lived,
Up and down and all around my friend.
Upside down, right side up,
I have not felt this way since I was a pup.
Sideways sidewalks, elongated stairs,
These are all images that make me stare.
Into the darkness, into the light,
One more time for our delight.
I can no longer see you over there,
You tell me to open my eyes too much to my surprise.
A surprise of life, a surprise of day,
Up and down does not make me afraid.
Fear is but a fleeting emotion that one cannot stop,
A black hole that you do not see but can make you drop.
A drop of water, a drop of the head,
Here comes that pesky - fear we all dread.
One more time I say,
Up and down does not make me afraid.

Photo by Anthony Delanoix on Unsplash.com

Emily in Paris

From the start, you stole my heart,
When you left that day, I gave it away.
One look in those beautiful eyes,
The City of Paris smiles.
Emily you are so bright, so cheerful, so free,
Upon your arrival, we didn't know what would be.
Falling in and out of love is what you do,
The City of Lights has been good to you.
You are growing in front of our eyes,
Taking what life brings, ready for every surprise.
Traveling the countryside, enjoying food and fine wine,
Revolutionizing the marketing world, one day at a time.
You are a fruit ripe for the picking; a sight for sore eyes,
An adventure ready to happen, a shooting star in the nighttime sky.
Your smile radiates and explains your pleasure,
Shining across the sky, like a hot air balloon floating by.
Soaring higher than you can even imagine,
Seen for miles and miles the whole day thru.
Quite the treasure, quite the treat,
You should never leave Paris, Please take your seat.
Think of all your new friends, your work, your opportunities,
All rolled up into one due to your bubbly personality.
You seem to come back for more,
You walk right thru that open door.
Looking for your true love in the city of lights,
Never considering compromising and never finding it satisfying.
Always moving forward, learning, loving, advertising,
It feels like you are in paradise, It feels like you are - Emily in Paris.

Picture by Cezar Sampaio on Unsplash.com

For the First Time

From the moment I met you I realized,
That you would be mine, until the end of time.
I glanced into those big baby blue eyes,
Much to my surprise, it had been far too much time.
Time to start a life together,
Time to start a family, a career, a partnership forever.
Now we are going on three, it occurred to me,
How special you are and how you make me feel.
When I am with you, I am floating on air; - I do not even care,
How can I stop but stare.
Whether we live in Cairo, London, or Paris,
It really does not matter, my dearest.
The most important thing to us all,
Is that we never shall never fall.
The call to care, to understand, to love with all our heart,
To forgive, to forget, and never forget our start.
You are the one and only, a one of a kind,
From start to finish, you blow my mind.
From here to there and back again,
Do not stop believing in us, from now to eternity in heaven...

Photo by Joel Rivera Camacho on Unsplash.com

Freedom

(The Fight for Liberties)
Freedom does not come for *free*,
Our Liberties may be in jeopardy.
This Marine may lose the battle, but win the war,
You are all Heroes that we appreciate more…
You keep us safe and tuck us in at night,
We take nothing for granted to make it right.
The right side of happiness, the right side of heaven,
We will always remember 911.
We cherish our warm beds and bow our heads,
For all the soldiers that have come before us.
Thank you for your service, all the blessings and delights,
We won't stop believing in our duty, our service, and our freedom,
For an eternity of nights.
Oorah!!!

Photo by Toa Heftiba on Unsplash.com

Hard to Understand

Every time I say no, you take control,
We need to take it really, slow.
I am looking up at you,
I see a future for two.
I know my bad habits drive you crazy,
I am trying to live my best life for you.
Whenever you look in the mirror,
You seem to always, disappear.
Remove those tears from your eyes,
May I come inside?
Your look defies everything I have inside,
Look up to the sky and figure out what you see in my eyes.
The Warmth you feel in your heart, sinks every time I walk away.
Do not worry I will only be gone away for a short time,
Every time you look my way, you really blow my mind.
This will not last forever, for this I am sure,
We only have so much time, so let us count every day.
Not just every day, but every minute, every breath, today.
This is one of life's delights,
One of many blessings, let us keep it true,
Forever me and you.

Photo by Kym Ellis on Unsplah.com

"Life is like riding
a bicycle,
To keep your balance,
You must keep moving."
-Albert Einstein

Have a Little Fun

You caught me in love again,
Don't you pretend that we are just friends.
You caught me in love again,
Let the wind blow your hair, like you don't care.
Take a little time to recover your mind,
Time to relax in the sunshine.
Just a hug, a squeeze, and a kiss to be pleased.
Just as there is no rhyme or reason to be pleasing all the time.
So buck up my friend, put on a smile, and have a little fun.
I feel like we just stepped off the dance floor.
My head is spinning, come and hold me close.
The music will never stop as long as we are together.
For today is a waltz, a slow dance, a toast.
For now and forever.

Photo by Zach Vessels on Unsplash.com

Hit the Door

This ain't your daddy's Chevorlet,
This ain't your cup of tea.
You are more than you can imagine,
You better leave right away…
You look at me with disgust in your eyes,
Do you really think I will take the time?
Do you really think this is a surprise?
Don't let the door hit you on the way out,
This is not the time to twist or shout.
Just get all your things and get OUT!

Photo by Rafi John Jimenez on Unsplash.com

HOLD ON TO ME

Hold on to the night,
Hold on until you can see,
Hold on to the memories,
Hold on to me.
Hold on tight,
Hold on with all your might,
Hold on for the ride of your life,
Hold on to what is in front of you,
Hold on and watch the view.
Hold on to the sights,
Hold on until you are free,
Hold on this is the key,
Hold on to the reverie.
Hold on and you will see,
Hold on to me,
Hold on as long as you can,
Hold on with both your hands.
Hold on so you don't fall,
Hold on and you will have it all,
Hold on and I will be your friend,
Hold on until the end.
Just hold on…

Photo by Antonio Gabola on Unsplash.com

Home Sweet Home (Alabama)-

by Will Reuhl

(My journey by land and sea)
When I land in Birmingham, The Greystone became my home.
It was my home away from home, my sweet home Alabama.
The membership is quite grand; Let me give you a hand...
One might say - you must get it right, before you are out of sight.
The site of Traditions is quite a sight.
Come check it out and walk about...
Your staff will serve you well,
You may even want to set a spell.
Just don't stand there empty handed,
There is always time for golf, tennis, swimming, or just hanging out - standing.
Watching the sunset on the terrace or dining al fresco was out of sight,
We continued with drinks and laughter throughout the night.
What made it even better was the Southern hospitality,
I say this was a perfect day at Greystone - Hooray!

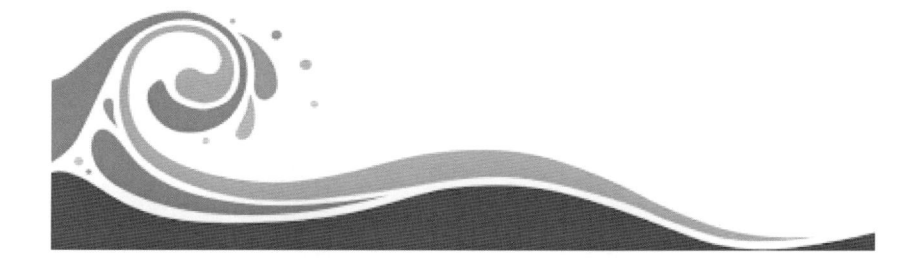

Photo by Max Saeling on Unsplash.com

Into the Night

I want you to feel safe in my arms,
Nothing should be faced alone or bring you harm.
As long as you sleep, close to me,
You will be safe, warm, and free.
To hold your head next to mine at night,
To tell you everything will be all right.
To wipe away all the tears from your face,
To wipe away all the fears without a trace.
Another night has come and gone,
We wake up with a smile at the dawn.
Stay with me and you will never be alone,
You have found your space, your new home.
Remove all that worry, all that pain,
Refresh the morning, and feel - you are sane.
Wake up every morning and do it again…
Look both ways before you cross the street,
Just take one-step at a time and create your own fate.
One baby step, one giant leap, keep moving straight.
Shoot for the stars, follow your heart, walk a straight path,
Whatever you do, do not lose faith,
Do not look back, move it forward, keep it straight.
Know at the end how hard you tried, you did your best,
Lay your head down at night and you will get some rest.
For the rest will take care of itself as long as you are next to me,
We will sleep sound, dream hard, and feel free.
Today, Tomorrow, and for Eternity…

Photo by Drew Colins on Unsplash.com

Last Dance

The way the moonlight dances from your eyes,
Makes me want to walk by your side.
There is no surprise in my mind,
This will last forever.
No matter what you say, we will always have today.
Walk with me, talk with me, here we go,
We are dancing to-and-fro, here and now, toe to toe.
The way you look at me, makes me feel this way.
Jump up and down - do not let me fall to the ground,
All I want to do is hold you now, so tight, and turn you around.
Love me, Live with me, Laugh with me.
We are on the rollercoaster ride of our life.
It is hard to escape, when your cape is only visible to these eyes.
You are my superhero, my pie in the sky, I always notice when you walk by…
Dance with me, Romance me; Take advantage of me.
You know what I want before I even know that I want it.
Do not try to force it, coerce it, but just stay the course with it.
Look out for the traffic light of life,
Just a little two -step to last through- out the night.
There is a kettle boiling on the stove,
It is brewing just for two like me and you!
We both know that will not be enough,
So take your best guess and wear that pretty dress.
Let us do what we do best, before this night's rest.
This could be our last dance, so let us make it last…

Photo by Michiel Com on Unsplash.com

Last Forever More

The way the moonlight dances from your eyes,
Makes me want to walk by your side.
There is no more surprise,
This will last forever more.
No matter what you say,
We will always have today.
Walk with me, here we go,
We are dancing to and fro.
The way you look at me,
Makes me feel that way.
Love me, Live with me, Laugh with me.
We are in this rollercoaster car together,
Just sit back and enjoy the ride.
It is so hard to escape,
When your cape is only visible to this Guy.
You are my super hero, my pie in the sky,
I do not want you to think of any other guy…
You are mine and I am yours,
I cannot think of anything so pure.
This is the time we need to concentrate,
Buy more time to perpetuate, make time to celebrate!
Do not forget me girl, I am right here,
For you, now and Forever more…

Photo by Adam Thomas on Unsplash.com

LONE STAR

In a land of Cowboys, Rangers, Mavericks, Astros, Stars, Rockets, and Bears,

There is a sheriff looking out for you, a marshall standing up for you, and a Texas Ranger defending you!

Women are friendly and pretty whether they live in the country or the city.

There is your trouble; You are seeing double.

Now go punch some cattle tonight.

Ice houses, roadhouses, courthouses; move from my house to your house, to her house.

No matter where you are; no matter what you do, it is all for you!

Walking in my shoes looking at the panoramic views,

Lightheaded and bed sweated -That is another point of view.

Sitting on my front porch swing, getting ready to sing to the radio,

A little country Western swing, playing my favorite song in spring.

I am singing, and no one is listening, moving like no one is watching,

Talking to myself, but not answering, enjoying every day of life...

Texas Stride	Texas Pride
Everyday	Everyway
Sunrise	to Sundown

Photo by Nick Fewings on Unsplash.com

Love Letter

My love for you grows stronger,
I am hoping to get to know you longer.
How young you feel is up to your heart,
I studied jazz, dance, and art.
I feel your energy and your heart,
Thinking of you makes my motor start.
Feeling forever young and always tearful,
Opening up, I am cautious and a little fearful.
It makes me cautious like a bird wrapping itself with its wings,
Before it leaves the nest with flight, it sings.
I am fascinated by the emotions you reveal in your words,
You express my love for you to the world.
If you were by my side now I would hug you tight,
Like the bird who continues to stay in the nest before flight.
I feel sad, will you share this emotion with me?
Like the butterfly when it flies free!
It is better to enjoy the moment and do whatever you want to do.
Remember the tree hole where we put the secrets we tell each other,
We know we are safe with one another.
Only the two of us know it exists,
A hole in the book full of emotion persists.
You have given me a lot of encouragement and love,
I want to be with you; it is a sign from above.
This is my lucky day too,
I am so happy I have met you.
I met the right person at the right time,
Every time I think of you, it blows my mind.
Let us meet in your dreams and in your mind,

Let us capture our love for all of mankind.
I am very happy and moved that you are thinking about me,
From the bottom of my heart, I wish you pleasant dreams.
Maybe the warmth of your love makes me sleepy,
Like a babies blanket wrapped tightly around as he is sleeping.
I am sure I will dream of you tonight,
Only you are in my head tonight.
We walk hand and hand on the soft grass,
The birds are singing for us, the flowers are blooming for us.
Our hearts help us make choices,
It beats faster and talks in voices.
Patience will give us more the moment we meet,
Like a flower opening in the spring of repeat.
You made me regain my confidence in Love,
You made me regain my trust in man and you.
You are like a ray of sunshine in my life,
You have removed all worries, all strife.
You melted my heart into a million drops of love,
We are not that far apart from rising above.
Truly beautiful people understand that beauty comes from within,
You are like a ray of sunshine in my Life, that is how I know this is Right.
You melted my HEART…
The mystery in us maybe what draws us to each other,
And when we fully understand we become family.
Are you in control of yourself now?
Striking a balance between work and Life?
You can't keep yourself so busy that you lose the details,
Know yourself better and leave open your sails.
Patience is a virtue, learning is important to move on,
Good morning love, I wish you were here to kiss me right now.
You are so funny, baby; you make me smile,

Come over here and lay with me for a while.
Okay, dear, let's plan together when I'm done with this time,
Spend each moment in your arms until the end of time.
Sleep well baby, you are so sweet,
If you were a candy bar, I would want to eat...
I wish I was by your side to make you breakfast baby,
Feeding you and bringing you hot water for tea, just you and me.
When I swim, I feel like a dolphin in a glass box,
Being released, back into the sea and flying free in the pool til three.
My favorite color is blue too.
When I stare at the blue sea or sky, it makes my thoughts slow down,
Blue represents melancholy, quietness, sanity, and calm.
Is this your yesterday?
You should take me there; you should take me to your special place.
Like me, I always do things with purpose and plan,
Like me, I like to be busy, charitable with time, and lend a hand.
When yield and ease of preservation are your primary destination,
This is just the beginning for us, we will write the story of the future together,
I feel your energy, your passion, and your smile at will.
Everything will happen naturally darling, it happens when the God of fate favors me,
I may be gone from your sight, but my heart is always there.
Hope is always bright, this is why the world will get better in my eyes.
Respect the World and everyone in it with a heart of learning,
Patience will give us more the moment we meet, even when you are yearning.
Keep shooting for the stars and settle for the moon, life illuminates your way.

IStock Photo on Unsplash.com

"It is love alone that gives worth to all things."
-Teresa of Avila

Love Letter Reply

(Here is my Response to your Love Letter)

Your eyes smile along with your lips,

I took you for a latte girl with a heart on the top of the cup.

An open heart and open mind can set you free,

Like an eagle soaring or a lion roaring, dream it and it will be.

Pride and humbleness are two great traits,

These traits separate success in many ways...

I am but your humble servant, a new friend sharing new ideas.

Cooperation in life is one of the keys to a good life,

It is what you have on the inside that counts the most!

Thank you for bringing me sunshine on a rainy day.

Thank you for your support and understanding today.

I wish we could have fireworks every night,

All our favorite things together would make this feel right.

You are very special to me; I like your style,

I will work by your side, play by your side,

Be honored to be on your side for every mile.

I am in love with life and in love with love,

I am in Love with you says the Lord from above.

You may be alone now and that is a choice you make,

My guess is that you will only be alone as long as it takes!

When you least expect it you will fall in love again,

Just stay open, stay positive, stay true, you must be happy with you.

You just need to be sure you are in love, that it is the real thing,

If that special person makes you better and you long for him, then ask for a wedding ring.

The important life lesson is to do what makes you happy,

To be in balance and create lasting memories.

You can ask me anything - your hopes, your dreams, you are everything.
If you are having a bad day, tell me, if something makes you laugh, tell me,
I am here for you, you have my full attention, you complete me.
You should not care what others think, be strong, you did nothing wrong.
Not everyone has the same timing in life, maybe you were promised gifts later in life,
No one can say, but stay open to the possibilities.
You are a good person with a good heart; we are in for a very good start.
I could not stop thinking about you; you were in my dreams,
We were swimming together, almost adjoined as one, it was simple fun.
My poetry is one of a kind, just like you,
I hope it resonates throughout your family and history too.
I will read to you all night and deep into the morning light,
I will read to you anytime you like.
My goodnight wish for you to sleep well, sleep tight, don't forget to turn out the light,
Do not stay up too late, do not take life as a free skate, and always kiss me goodnight.
There are many miles between us but my heart still longs for you,
My mind longs for you, I have grown very fond of you - Yet, here we are alone.
I am heading off to bed early tonight after a late night last night,
I will dream of you all night long and there will be nothing wrong.
You are a hard one to forget, you are always on my mind,
Today, tomorrow, and until the end of time.
I hope you will dream of me hugging you all night long,
The kind of hug that warms you inside, the kind of hug that makes love on the right side.
The number one lesson in a relationship is good communication,
A couple needs to be able to express themselves to one another.
Bad communication is like a ship without its rudder, you never get anywhere,
Hopelessly going in circles on the boat of life, which will never get you anywhere.
Open communication and unconditional love,
No matter how hard it is, we need to talk about it.

The bottom line is that I want to love you on a higher level,

To know you better than any other fellow.

Please continue to share more about you, likes and dislikes the whole day thru.

It is important to try to understand each other,

If we say something, what does it really mean? Will it get us farther?

You are the sunshine, you are my light, you are my desire, my delight.

What we have is special, what we have will last forever,

What we have is fate, wisdom, and knowledge more than ever.

Imagine me touching you, imagine you touching me, dream of me,

Tonight is but a time to rest in order to start another day fresh and into my arms.

There is love in the air, there is love everywhere,

Where we walk and when we talk, and always when we are together,

I take your hand and you will understand how special you are.

Hold on tight because we are gonna make love all night.

You make me feel young and alive, wanted and loved,

I liked to think I am wiser today than yesterday, but it is still fun to share.

Try not to think of me too much today,

We found each other at the right time of year in spades.

You are giving me more purpose in life; I see the good in you,

Do not drive without your seatbelt or take your eyes off the road,

This is but a road less traveled in the great journey of life.

Some days will mean more than others,

Just remember, I am always thinking about you being a mother.

My arms are outstretched halfway around the world,

I am hoping you can feel my love for miles and miles,

Our souls and hearts are becoming intertwined,

So let's continue to plan to be together and hold each other tight, today and until eternity.

I know you are right, but it helps to get reassurance from you,

I love your kind words, You make me feel special and loved.

I feel fireworks go off every time I talk to you,

It is like the Fourth of July every day, and I won't lie.

I am not the most patient, so you will have to be patient for two,

All I can do is try to make it the best for you.

This will be another stairway to climb for all of time,

If I had your smile, I would be happy all the time.

I look at your pictures and all I want to do is look you in the eyes and kiss your lips.

That feeling you get when you are floating in the sea or the way you look at me.

I philosopher once said to make time for the things you love,

You stimulate my mind, not just my body.

You are so exciting to me; I can't stop messaging you.

We will never get tired of each other; we have a lot to share,

Like a violin playing a concerto, my love grows...

How about I sing, and we dance together throughout this special night,

Every night could be like this from morning till night.

So Dance with me, romance with me, stare at me, do anything you want to me,

I am yours now, and forever my darling, for as far as you can see.

Can you feel your heart racing, my smile growing, the earth moving, the floor shaking,

My hugs getting tighter, my lips getting softer, my kisses sweeter, our relationship making?

Touch me again, dance with me again, don't you pretend, we are both enjoying this till the end.

Your eyes and head are getting heavy against mine, Now fall asleep in my arms,

Listen to music, feel the dreams, nothing bad will happen, there will be no harm.

I will whisper in your ears sweet nothings in the night; I will say I love you each and every night,

I will kiss your ear with delight, as we lay under that bright moonlight.

Every time we talk I want to be with you more, to feel your touch,

My body quivers for your warm embrace.

I miss the taste of your sweet lips, I miss the way you hold me on our trip,

I miss you more and more each and every day, You are my sun, my moon, my whole day.

I said you have a smile in your eyes, maybe it's a rainbow of surprise,

A pure spark of happiness in your heart, the kind that creates that spark.

Maybe they sparkle like a diamond in the sky or shining on a snow - covered mountainside.

Your lips are like cherry wine, sweeter than mine, they are so fine,

I nearly blow my mind, we need to find more time.

Loving you is like a dream come true, a little piece of heaven for me and you.

Before we met my life was missing something and I had no idea that I was missing you,

You continue to energize me each and every day, both my mind and my body!

If we always express our feelings, our relationship will grow,

Like a flower in the garden of life, our love will grow.

Are we heading the right direction?

Are you comfortable with our conversations?

Keep no secrets, tell no lies. Have I lost you, darling, in the sky?

At the end of the day, that is all I can ask, to kiss each other good night and have no regrets.

Have I not told you how beautiful you are tonight?

If I were there now, I would hold you tight and kiss you all night.

Hug and squeeze you until daylight…

That is one of the things that makes me love you even more - your patience and kindness!

Our story has just begun, each chapter is being written. Who knows how the story will end.

Did you know that a goldfish only has a five second memory?

When something bad happens in life, we need to be a goldfish: react, process, learn, and move on.

The reason I love history is we can learn from the past to help us in the future!

If we pay close attention, we will not make the same mistake twice.

Stay open to life, keep learning and it will be all right. Be alive!

In the expanse of time, we are only here a short time.

Enjoy every breath and keep smiling all the day thru,

Positivity is powerful, it is infectious, it is True.

It is always right, for me and you.

You are a breath of fresh air in the evening sky; you are the one who caught my eye,

See that beautiful sunset? That reminds me of you and I!

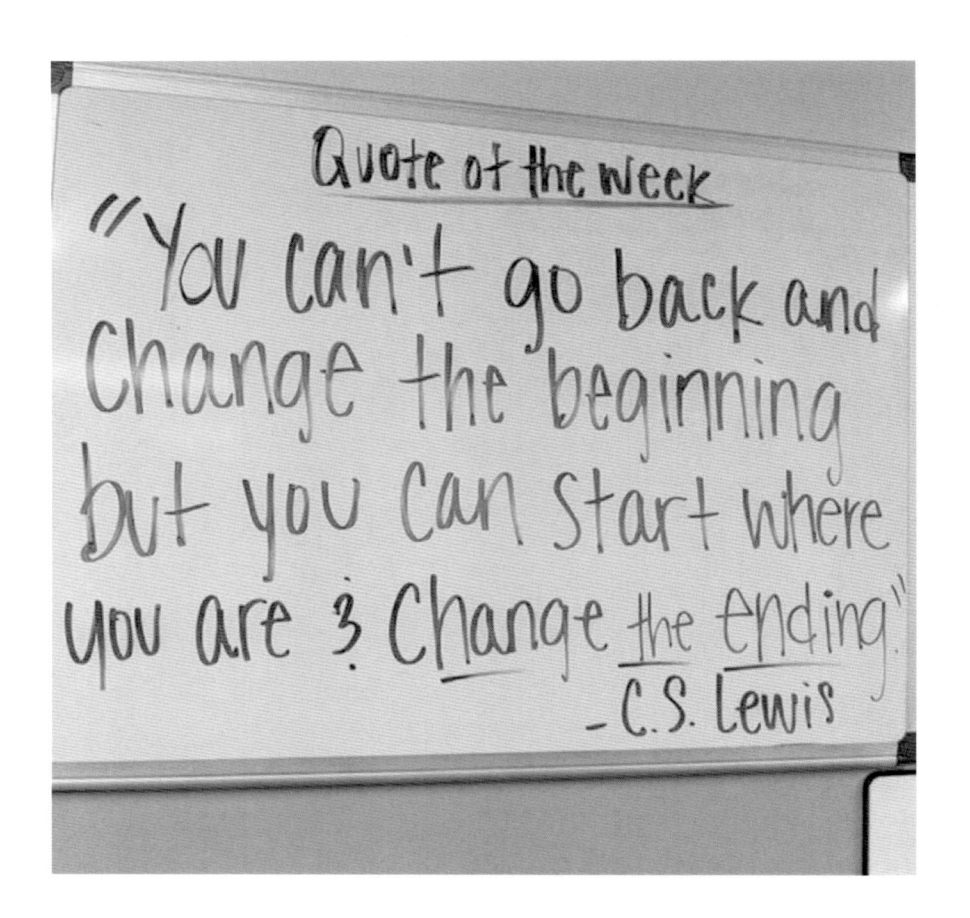

Istock photo on Unsplash.com

Photo by Johannes Plenio on Unsplash.com

"Happiness is when
What you think,
What you say,
And what you do
Are in harmony."
-Mahatma Gandhi

Photo by Ryan Franco on Unsplash.com

Love Struck

You caught me in love again, just like the other men.
Do not pretend that we are just friends?
You caught me in love again.
Let the wind blow your hair like you don't care,
Left behind, stuck in a chair.
Let the earth move below your feet,
Left of center until the day of defeat.
Take a little time, time to relax in the sunshine.
Just a hug, squeeze, and a kiss to be pleased,
There is no rhyme or reason to be pleasing all the time.
So buck up Chuck, put on that smile, and jump on that dance floor.
Show some style, and have some fun for a while.
My head is spinning, come and hold me close.
The music will never stop as long as we are together.
For today is a Waltz,
Tomorrow a Toast,
The Future will be a boast.
For Now and Forever,
AMEN.

Photo by Ja San Miguel on Unsplash.com

Me and Tucker

As I sit here with each passing moment,
I wonder what it would be like to be man's best friend.
To get up each morning, go outside, do my business,
Eat my breakfast, and get a ride...
My day bed is up against the wall,
Maybe I will chew on my bone, or stand by the door and stall.
Everyone is sitting at the table,
I decide to chillax and pretend I am in some kind of a fable.
Maybe I am the King's steed or a mere court taster,
I close my eyes and dream of simpler times.
If I taste the king's food one more time,
My eyes will get large as I sit by his side.
To grab that turkey leg and play tug of war with his majesty,
I of course let him win, where do I begin?
Soon enough I wake as Hank may arise,
We get up and go outside, maybe another ride?
As I return inside, I realize how lucky I am,
I smile and enjoy every stroke from my master.
How many can be at cabin, loved unconditionally,
With the ability to lay around all day long...
I nod, look for more attention, smile again, and return to my routine.
The sun shines upon me and keeps me warm,
I never have to sleep alone.
How blessed am I to be with my best friend,
From now until the Bitter End.

Photo by Jon Tyson on Unsplash.com

Moving Up or Moving Out

Owning my presence to improve my disgrace,
In control of my essence by adding loves embrace.
Must I be part of the human race,
Or find myself with a heart at race.
This is so hard to face,
I must look hard or perhaps erase.
Erase my memory from the fear or the pain,
That it might come again.
Millions of people enter the waters creating their own waves,
With mothers and fathers becoming impervious with one another.
Lest us not put asunder, What God said to others,
We must try hard to live a good life and treat others well.
Circumstances that add to God's presents,
Is a gift to the whole human race.
I love that you love me,
And that you love that I love you.
I wish you nothing but happiness,
And happiness will find you.
I hope everything goes well,
And your well is filled with everything.
This must include hope, faith, and charity,
And the greatest of these is Love.
So says the Bible, So says the Lord.
Who among us will trust us, prevail us, ensure us,
Activate us, enthrall us with unbiased non combust!

My hope is for your love to become my love,

My happiness your happiness,

This is where two become one.

Do not just follow the sun, but be aware of everyone.

This love must be true,

It is my wish for you.

To grow old with one another,

Hold on tight to one another.

Respect and understand one another.

For not just today or tomorrow but for eternity.

For we are stronger together than apart,

This is a brand new start.

The light that you share is plain to see,

Just look at all the birds and the trees.

Look towards the sky and the sunshine,

Never turn the corner to a blind eye.

For life is not a straight road,

Life is not empty as long as you hold.

Hold on for all the curves and up and downs,

Never let anyone say that you were unfound.

Climb the mountain of life together,

Not just today but forever.

Forever in your mind, forever in your heart,

Forever as a couple, forever as one.

This is my Gift to You,

Always have fun as two...

Happiness

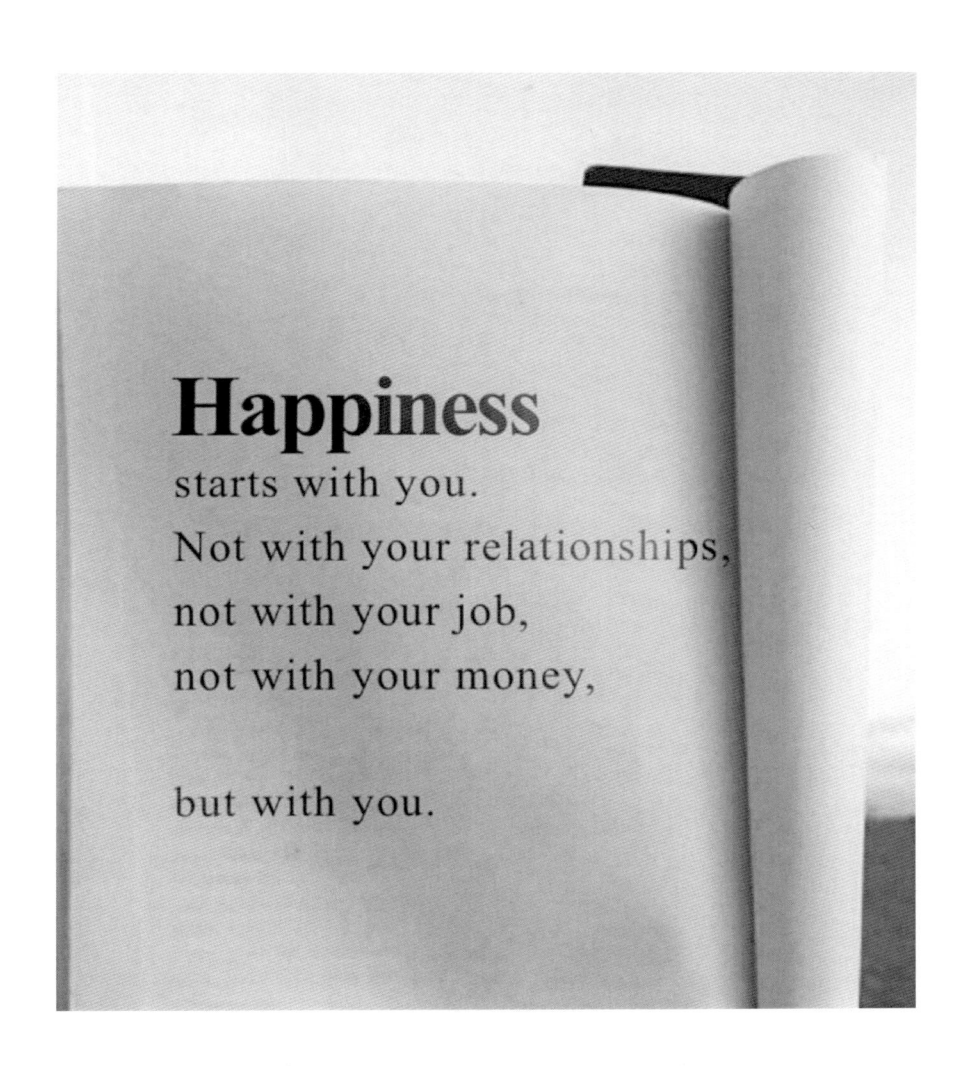

starts with you.
Not with your relationships,
not with your job,
not with your money,

but with you.

Istock Photo on Unsplash.com

Photo by Yuichi Kageyama on Unsplash.com

My Little Butterfly

I float, I flutter, I fly,
Oh, my little Butterfly.
I am orange and black,
Yellow and black,
Even blue or greens,
No matter what color, I will follow my dreams.
My job is to fly from flower to flower and pollinate,
Sometimes I have to wear glasses to see straight.
I lean to the left, I lean to the right,
Sometimes I stand in the middle and cast a big shadow.
When I grow up space exploration is on my list,
Only encouragement, no discouragement, I must persist.
To see the stars, the moon, a planet,
I need to study, read, calculate, and plan it.
The first woman astronaut to Mars is my goal,
To fly here to there and be America's hero.
Even if I never leave the ground,
My theory will be very sound.
Like the butterfly, I will spread my wings,
To become and imagine anything.
I will brighten every room I enter,
With colors that are not always in the center.
I will look for that silver- lining in everything I do,
I look at my bright future and stay in school.
Learning is but an option and opportunity is at every turn,
I shall learn from my mistakes and always keep my glass half- full.
It is really up to all of us to stay positive and grow,
Like the butterfly, we will discover which way to go...

Photo by Matthew Ronderseith on Unsplash.com

My Old Yellow Jeep

Have you ever gone four wheeling after a rain?
Or gotten stuck on the tracks by a train?
Or put the top down and let your hair flow?
How about going so fast, that you did not even know?
Have you ever been pulled over for not making a complete stop?
Or had to rebuild a carburetor or a suspension late at your shop?
Have you ever had too much fun in your old yellow Jeep?
Or filled the seats with too many, where you could not see out?
Or rolled down the windows with the radio too loud and shout?
What about a full moon seen through the window on a sunny day?
Or a flower displayed on the dash in the month of May?
How do I learn to drive a stick with no one around?
Or pick up my boss up at the airport without a sound?
Do you feel free when driving on down the road?
Or fall asleep after driving a long distance all alone?
Have you ever kissed a girl in the front seat during a rain storm?
Or cuddled in the back seat at a drive-in movie while you brain stormed?
Is it true that everything is more fun in your old yellow jeep?
At night, do you dream about driving with your girlfriend before you fall asleep?
Is your dream over at the next light when someone decides to beep?
Or are you waiting for next year's model or maybe a new Jeep?
Does it have to break down or end the fun too soon?
After all, you want to ride up to the lake, maybe in late June?

"Learning never exhausts the mind." — *Leonardo da Vinci*

Photo by Geio Tischler on Unsplash.com

"Logic will get you from A to B Imagination will take you everywhere."
-Albert Einstein

Next Jen

I stayed up late last night waiting for your call and it never came,
I needed to know if we are strangers or still friends.
It may not happen now; it may not happen then,
It may not happen tomorrow; it may not happen at all.
I am still holding out and wondering how?
There may be too many miles between us to overcome,
Both in Age and on the road, it may lead to no more fun.
You were my muse, my joy, my instant friend,
I thought our relationship was growing until the end.
I do not know what happened, I cannot deny,
I just want to look into your eyes that night with a big surprise.
To touch you, hold you, caress you, hug you,
I wanted you to know how much I cared for you...
Not just today or tonight or tomorrow without flight,
But the day after, and the next day after that, in full sight.
Getting others to know and approve may be our best move,
It may never happen or improve; we may have to wait for the next full moon.
Time is not on our side, our family and friends may not understand,
Our love must grow and hang on to each other's hand, a strong base will withstand.
Is this goodbye? Should I call you later? Is this the End?
Look all around and keep your head up high,
I am sure you will find the right Guy.
So make your decision it should not be this hard,
It is either written or it is not in the cards.
Say good night and sleep well; sure thoughts and pleasant dreams, it is a sure tell of what maybe.

Photo by Crystal Huff on Unsplash.com

No Flowers, No Rain

A young woman had a tattoo on each leg,
It read: No Flowers, No rain.
I told her there was a poem in there, somewhere,
And you could read it reaching out from there.
Are there flowers without rain?
Is there a path to take in vain?
How can you stop without a gain!
I am not sure just call out my name...
Is it better for the sun or the rain to bounce upon your home?
Is it better for your whole body to work out and call your own?
I have been to the mountain top and looked down,
I have felt the rain on my face and all around.
The wind in my hair and the sun reflecting from the window,
All for that one chance to say, you cannot go.
We are different from the wild animals and more,
We know when to get out of the rain and when to hit the door.
Do not let the door hit you from behind,
When you know it is right there on your mind.
Just move ahead and do not look back,
Because despite it all you should not attack.
Just slide back and observe it all,
Take it all in and do not let yourself fall.
Just listen to those and understand,
Life is worth living, somewhat forgiving, and shared by man.

"Education breeds confidence. Confidence breeds hope. Hope breeds peace."
- Confusius

Photo by Alexandre Debieve on Unsplash.com

No Way Out

Get out, pull out,
Fall out, come out.
Be out, just out,
Hold out, sold out.
Fold out, hide out,
Shut out, buy out.
Figure out, black out,
Close out, white out.
Shout out, flight out,
Side out, I'm out.
Walk out, tide out,
Jury out, slide out.
Camp out, Run out,
Scoot out, lose out.
Search out, bring out,
Speak out, locked out.
My out, You're out,
Call out, Peace out.

Photo by Nathan Dumlao on Unsplash.com

"Where words fail, Music SPEAKS"
-Hans Christian Andersen

One Latte'

Just sitting in Chappie's Café,
Sipping on my hot latte'.
Hey, you're kinda cute, do you want to dance with me?
I promise, that won't be you last time you drink for free!
Lookin out at the mountainside or a quiet stream,
That look in your eyes as if this is a dream.
Let's walk out of here and see if this is our best year.
If not, we will have no regret,
Just a pure reaction to the attraction - Don't you fret.
Sit there and look into my eyes; I am totally focused on you.
Your flowing hair, your gypsy stare, the sun glowing from your eyes.
I must be dreamin', this must have meaning; we have nothing but time.
All of a sudden, you're away, without a word that day,
Will I remember you? Was this a dream come true?
Come a little closer before you leave. I want to whisper in your ear.
This is our year; you have nothing to fear.
Leave me your number, and I will call you soon,
How about before noon or this June?
I must see if there is more before I hit the door.
Thanks a Latte' for joining me today,
It was so nice to meet you - Good day...

Photo by Ismail Hamzah on Unsplash.com

One Lens, One Picture, One Time

An aperture in the lens of your mind,
Makes me picture you in one space and one time.
Are you out of focus or just slow to change,
Are you afraid you will lose your way?
Is it time for change,
Or is it time to rearrange.
Capture that moment with a nod or a smile,
The right light or a song to pass time bye.
Do you need a reason why?
I will explain it in one hundred years or less,
Are these words even blessed for less?
How do you measure success?
Did you just undress your importance,
Miss your flight, in a lifetime of romance?
Record as many memories if you can,
Not just the dreams of one man.
Reach for the stars, settle for the charms,
Your life is more precious than you can harm.
I shot an arrow in the air and where it landed, I did not care.
As long as you get it, shoot it, capture it, remember it, and more.
You will land it at the right time,
Have that right feeling in your mind,
Know when you are right, if not all the time.
I will always remember my first child, my first camera, my first photo, my first kiss.
One movie, one night, one unforgettable lifetime,
A moment in time, one large moment of bliss...

Photo by Caleb Jones on Unsplash.com

Pelican Port Resort

It was the first week of summer and school had just gotten out. It is time to load the station wagon with six kids and a dog. We are making the annual trek to Northern Minnesota. The drive will take us about twelve hours. My brother, Rob, and I get the way back because we are the smallest. My youngest sister, Judy, would sometimes join us in the way back or squeeze into the back seat with my other three sisters, Linda, Nancy, and Sandy. My parents sat in the front and our toy - miniature poodle, Angel, would roam between all the seats! My parents would put a large, yellow - foamed matt the length of the way back and all our luggage was on top of the car. We looked like the Griswald's from the movie "Vacation". We would pack the car the night before and get up at the break of dawn to leave around 5 a.m. The goal was to get to the resort before dark. There were a lot of things we didn't know back in the 1960's and 70's, like not wearing seat belts or my parents smoking in the front and my brother and sisters inhaling second - hand smoke. We all somehow survived. Looking back, those were some of the best times of my life! Of course, you can imagine, there was heavy traffic, construction, and storms along the way. There were many sibling arguments ("Are we there yet"), rosaries said, and lots of sleeping. You betcha. In the 60's there were no tollways, superhighways- just two lane highways! Today, you make that same drive in about eight hours (still a long day, but worth it). My father would drive us up at the beginning of summer, spend a week with us, and then he would go back to Chicago to go to work for the next two months. Then in August, he would return for a two - week vacation, and then the whole family would take to the road to return home. The drive was not the best. However, our greatest memories were made "Up North." We were very lucky because my grandparents, Grama Re (short for Marie) and Pop, owned a Resort on a lake where we stayed for the entire Summer! Oh yes, Pelican Port Resort, my grandparents pride and joy! The resort, itself, was made up of five cabins and a main house. They rented out four of the cabins and my family occupied cabin number five all Summer, every summer for the first seventeen years of my life (1960-1977). We even got to leave most of our summer stuff in the cabin year round because cabin number five was never rented. We had constant bonfires, birthday parties, family reunions, and barbeques. The main house was in the middle front, closest to the lake, and the cabins started to the right of the main house and went in a half – circle, finishing to the left of the main house (like a horseshoe). Inside the horseshoe was an open area where all the parties took place, a kind of central compound. The gravel road to get into the resort ran down next to cabin three and went in a circle to each cabin with a grassy area in the middle. That grassy area was what I called the central compound. There was room between each cabin to park your car. Included in the rent, every cabin received a numbered row boat for the week. Each cabin was normally rented for a week, Saturday to Saturday, but there was an exception to every cabin, except cabin number two, after 1970. In 1970, my mom's sister, Billie Lu and husband, Tom, and my 5 cousins purchased cabin number three! Cabin number one was rented by my other grandparents, Grama Lu and Grandpa Joe for the entire Summer. Cabin number four was rented by my grandmother's cousin, Joe Mirabella and his wife. The resort was literally, a family affair! Cabin number two was rented by the same people for the same week, every year. Over the years, cabin number two renters became like family. Back then, I thought I ran the place! When I was old enough to walk, I would help my Pop clean the row boats, tie the boats to the dock, and welcome the guests to the resort. I know Pop never paid me but Grama Re would slip me a dollar or two when he wasn't looking! This was an Ultra-Modern resort, which means it has in-door plumbing. A lot of the first cabins up north had outhouses for bathrooms and a hand pump to get your water from a well. Most of the wells were spring fed, like the lakes, which produced clean, clear, delicious water. Big Pelican Lake had a sand bottom where you could see 8-10 feet deep down to the bottom. The only problem is that a spring fed lake is cold, but you would get used to it. Believe it or not, I was never up there in the winter, when it would get below zero and the lake would freeze solid. Solid enough to drive your car on it! So, I have never ice fished (on my bucket list). By August the water would warm up quite a bit but was still refreshing on a hot summer day. The fishing was always good, especially earlier in the summer.

    Once it got hot, the fish went deeper and were harder to find. We knew every inch of that lake and could always find the fish. That is until millions of other people discovered the lake and pulled out too many fish! The lake has not been as good of a fishing lake in recent years but continues to be one of the premiere recreational lakes in Minnesota.

    One could say I grew up on the lake because I spent almost three months a year there. Up North, I learned how to fish, boat, ski, swim, and make sand castles. I will never forget rising early in the morning to hunt for frogs. The frogs would gather under the row boats, which were tied up on shore at night. We would collect the frogs and sell them to the local bait shop, Marv Koep's, for 10-25 cents each. We would then take the money to the corner store and spend our earnings on candy, soda, and ice cream. The corner store was located on the North shore, about a half hour walk on the sand, from where we were on the south shore. Not only did we love to walk along the shoreline, but you could walk out two hundred yards from shore until the water was over your head. This made the south shore great for swimming as a child. All the moms would be sitting in the water with their lawn chairs, while we kids were splashing around in the water and playing in the sand with plastic army men and Matchbox cars. We also had plastic toy boats that we would play with in the lake. We would pull some sand back from shore making a semi- circle, where the water could get in, but not get out. We would put our toy boats in this, like a homemade harbor. Of course, we had sand pails and shovels to help build giant sand castles and we would build roads and moats around the castles. We spent every sunny, hot summer day at the beach. Unfortunately, there was no sun - tan lotion back then, either. This gave a lot of us sunburns at times and lots of wrinkles as we get old. However, I would not change a thing! Pelican Lake was a good fishing lake. The best thing about fishing was not only about catching a big fish, but eating it afterward at one of our famous fish fries! My mom would take crushed saltine crackers and eggs and use them to fry up the best tasting fish you have ever eaten. I learned how to catch fish, so we could eat them! My brother, father, and grandfather would spend hundreds of hours every summer catching fish, fileting them, and then eating them! I became good at all that revolved around fishing. The easiest fish to find, even to this day, is the large mouth bass. They come into the shallows at night to feed near shore in the weed beds. We would get up early ever morning and catch lots of bass. My two favorite things in life are bass fishing and dancing, both skills my father taught me (Thanks again Dad). I found that fishing over the years was much more fun out of a boat! Early on all the row boats were wood, but eventually they were made of heavy aluminum. Other than the traditional three seat row boat, there were lots of pontoons, cris - craft, and speed boats on the Lake. The pontoon wasn't just a great fishing boat but it was a great cocktail cruiser during happy hour in the evenings. We even dressed up the pontoon for the annual 4th of July water parade! The fireworks that appeared over the largest lake resort was epic, and my cousins always found a way to bring up their own fireworks every year. Fabulous, fun fireworks...

  I have been returning to Pelican Lake for the last sixty-two years straight! My children and now my grandchildren have experienced it too. Everyone enjoys the water, sun, and fresh air Up North. When it comes to fishing, we are working on our fifth generation of fishermen. My grandchildren are learning to fish and when they are teenagers they will learn to filet and cook fish. Bass fishing, Up North, is rather one dimensional. We use a bait cast with a weedless hook and a live minnow. You cast high up in the air towards the weeds creating a big splash! The splash creates a ring on the water which sends a message to the bass that it is feeding time. We then start reeling slowly to create the illusion that the minnow is swimming away. The bass chases the minnow and bites it. The fishing line tugs and you set the hook by pulling back swiftly and start to reel in. You want to reel quick enough to keep the fishing line taught and out of the weeds. Once the clear the weeds, the fish will swim up and jump out of the water trying to spit out the hook. Seeing a bass jump is one of the most exciting things about fishing. It is a beautiful sight. You reel the fish into the boat and then tie it on a nylon rope stringer, attached to the boat, and let the fish back in the water to swim. You have caught the equivalent of two filets. If we catch three more, we have enough for a family fish fry. If we have a lucky week, we will catch enough for 2-3 meals! Besides swimming and playing in the sand, boating is the next attractive thing that we enjoy.

  Every year we have access to a pontoon boat, which will fit the whole family. We will explore the lake extensively fishing, touring, exploring Islands, anchoring, and swimming, and, of course fishing. If we are lucky, we will even go skiing or tubing behind the boat. This is a highlight, especially for the non-fisherman, which consists of my wife and grandchildren under three! When we were kids, the thrill was being old enough to swim out to the raft, which was placed in about 5-6 feet of water. Not only was the raft a great place to suntan, but we would play king of the hill, sink half the raft and jump off, and even skinny dip at night on the raft. We all loved the water. Our moms loved the water because it would wear us out so it was easier to get us to sleep. Nap in the afternoon when we were young or go to bed by 9-10pm when we got older. Growing up on a lake you learned a lot: take care of the engine on the boat by keeping away from logs, heavy weeds, or running out of gas; watching out for storms, which you could see blowing across the water; and water safety. We would always swim in pairs and wear a life jacket on the boat. I will never forget this one storm where my Grandpa Joe and I stayed too long on the water. We were literally racing the storm to shore. I jumped out of the boat, tied it tight to the dock, and preceded to run to the cabin. Not two minutes after we got in the cabin a great boom struck behind us with a great burst of light. Lightning had struck a tree, not two feet from where we just were, splitting a forty foot tree in half! There was a burst of flame and then the heavy rain extinguished it, and it began to smoke heavily. This is why you don't stand under a tree in a lightning storm. A good lesson learned.

If it rained it was time to play board games, puzzles, or go into town shopping. If we saved our frog money or allowance we got to buy a toy or book in town. Also it was a family tradition that my Pop would bring us into town every year to buy us moccasins (Native American handmade leather shoes that we wore as slippers). Going to town was a treat because the only time we went there was when it rained or was cloudy (not a beach day or too windy to fish). The town had a candy and iced cream store, a little donut stand, pizza restaurant, A&W root beer restaurant, breakfast diner, marina shop, The pickle factory (one of two bars in town), several clothing boutiques, and two toy stores called the Totem Pole and Zaisers. I not only ran the resort, but I knew all the owners of the stores! How did I know everyone? Well, my grandparents did not only own a resort, they also owned a clothing store, called Town & Lake. Town & Lake was right between the diner and Zaisers! My father was an only child and my grandfather loved to walk us kids around town showing us off every year. My grandfather and the owner of the Totem Pole came up with this idea for turtle races in downtown every Wednesday afternoon in the summer to attract tourists into downtown Nisswa. The turtle races did the job attracting hundreds of people to downtown every Wednesday. My brother and I were one of the first racers. My children and now grandchildren have raced turtles! My grandparents eventually sold the resort but kept the store in the family. My parents ran the store until 1987 and then sold it. My parents lived in Minnesota until my dad passed in 2014. My middle sister is the only Reuhl still living up there to this day. The only significant change to Nisswa over the years is the amount of Championship golf courses. An additional attraction. In 1908, Mr. Leon Lum suggested that the township of Smiley should be renamed Nisswa, a word derived from the Ojibwa tribe "nessawae" meaning "in the middle," or "three." This was and still is a great place to spend time, especially in the summer.

Photo by Nathan Dumlao on Unsplash.com

Perfect Day

The past is never gone, it is never forgotten, it is just not yet found,

Open your eyes, keep moving forward, don't look back at mistakes, don't get unwound.

Looking out the window pane of my heart,

It is clear to me that you see pain that has started.

Look and you shall see the pain within,

The soul crying into the wind.

Bow down and reflect what went wrong,

But don't take too long to see right from wrong.

We know what we want, but sometimes do not know how to get there,

We know what to do and when to do it without constant fanfare.

We reach the highest mountain, swim the deepest sea,

Travel all around the world, just to get back to thee.

We seek a peaceful solution, an inner peace,

Just a deep understanding of what was meant to be.

Can you see the plan?

Can you appreciate the perfect day?

Maybe you need to hear the message and see what is right in front you today,

Do you settle when things do not go your way.

Are you afraid to apologize, are you afraid to realize,

Don't delay, Haste makes for lies, tragedy, and pain.

Express yourself with random acts of kindness, even if it rains.

Pull in the reins of your mistakes, please do not hesitate,

Your missteps, your misdemeanors, your missed attempts as of late.

These are the bars of life which separate are thoughts from our madness,

Our words from our actions, our good from evil, our happiness from sadness.

Walk that straight line in your mind full of optimization of all times...

Photo by Toa Heftiba on Unsplash.com

Random Rhymes

Attention, apprehension, appreciation,

Frustration and unification.

Prevails, rails, trails, sails.

Risk, mix, fix, wicks, and sticks.

Matters, flatters, patterns of discouragement.

Reaching out without a doubt.

Not knowing what you will find on the other side.

Appearing, fearing, tearing, and searing.

From the rising, to the surprising, to the setting of the sun,

We have fun, when we run, in the sun.

This is my son, the only one, the right, when you thought it was wrong.

Tables in fables, baubles and fobbles, one and done.

Name, fame, blame, game.

Truth, youth, tooth, in a phone booth?

My motion is your emotion in the commotion of that potion.

I was taken upon my wake in this awaken, to what is at stake.

My solution in that institution was a mutation of jubilation.

You must hide to shine, beside the intertwined.

That flight could cause a bite in the night of fright,

Ain't that right? There were slugs and bugs under rugs in clubs.

We spread the bed spread on the bed near the head by the crumbs of bread.

I gasped at the grasp of the clasp upon your wrist that was in a fist of mist.

If you set a while it may be in style upon a pile of riches in bed.

It is fine if you climb the slime of my rhymes in due time.

The pilot knew if he with-drew the climate would see through the cloud,

Around the earthbound vessel until noon or around the earth and moon.

The mission's fruition was compounded at every turn.

Photo by Shane Rounce on Unsplash.com

Ready, Aim, Higher

When you spend most of your life in one industry does it make you invaluable?

Let us say you were stuck in an elevator for hours with someone you did not know,

Does this make it so or artificially make you get to know these things that you did not know.

Slow down and carefully think thru that which gives it value,

When all is said and done, make sure it is done in a kind way.

Why is no one hiring me?

Why does no one care?

I am alone in this space, floating, sitting within my despair.

Is it my Age, my Experience, my hair?

How can someone be worth so much one day and worthless the Next?

I always wonder what could have been or what could be,

What really matters to one does not matter to all.

Is an interview the ultimate test?

Do you need to ace this test to be in demand?

Whatever happened to fairness, the golden rule, and human dignity?

What happened to treating someone as your equal,

To guide, teach, and lead by example...

"We all have ability. The difference is how we use it."– Stevie Wonder

Photo by Keenan Kitchen on Unsplash.com

"You miss 100 percent of the shots you don't take."
-Wayne Gretzky

RIDGEWOOD WAY

Ridgewood way, Ridgeway way, it really happens every day, it's Ridgewood way...

Halfway between Dallas and Austin way, doesn't matter what you say, it's Ridgewood way...

This is a ditty about you and me with a special mention of "Ridgewood"- That makes Three!

Arrive on horseback or by car, it really doesn't matter where you are.

This is a country song, so you may want to sing along.

Whether living on the hillside overlookin' or being around the corner, and good lookin'.

Just set a spell, and you will know me well, that is the Ridgewood way.

Ridgewood way, Ridgeway way, it really happens every day, it's Ridgewood way...

Halfway between Dallas and Austin way, doesn't matter what you say, it's Ridgewood way...

Food that afternoon melted in your mouth, with the Chef cookin', it was the best on the couch.

It was a simple mix of olive oil, salt and pepper, with a little demi-glaze, - The flavors were so good, it created a purple haze.

It was a rainy day with good company; great food, great drinks, and a playful way -That is the Ridgewood way.

Ridgewood way, Ridgeway way, it really happens every day, it's Ridgewood way...

Halfway between Dallas and Austin way, doesn't matter what you say, it's Ridgewood way...

Ridgewood has tennis, golf, swimming, boating, and the like, positioned on Lake Waco, you can run into the night.

This year's member-guest tournament went without a hitch,

Everyone was so excited including Bill, Stewart, and Mitch.

Hey everybody - That's the Ridgewood way!

Ridgewood way, Ridgeway way, it really happens every day, it's Ridgewood way...

Halfway between Dallas and Austin way, doesn't matter what you say, it's Ridgewood way...

Chip and Joanna were nowhere in sight; I only saw a few magnolia's before my flight.

Round and round I go, another splash into the pool - to and fro.

Even the slide on the boat was empty, but we didn't mind,

They say you can see "42" on the eighteenth hole from time to time. That's the Ridgewood way.

Ridgewood way, Ridgeway way, it really happens every day, it's Ridgewood way...

Halfway between Dallas and Austin way, doesn't matter what you say, it's Ridgewood way...

So, the next time you're in Waco or by the lakeside, make sure to stop by Ridgewood for a good time.

You will never forget it, It will blow your mind...

Moving back and forth, again and again, forever and ever - AMEN. That is the Ridgewood way...

Ridgewood way, Ridgeway way, it really happens every day, it's Ridgewood way...

Halfway between Dallas and Austin way, doesn't matter what you say, it's Ridgewood way...

"Only in the darkness can you see the stars."
-Martin Luther King, Jr.

Photo by Ian Keefe on Unsplash.com

Photo by Coral Ouellette on Unsplash.com

Rocky Mountain High

The stars were out that night on full display,
They wanted to know if you could come out and play.
The entire sky lit up with delight,
You can almost touch them as they took flight.
The night was clear as far as you could see,
We heard coyotes howling from behind the trees.
The start of a feast one coyote said,
He called all his friends until the prey was dead.
We lit a bonfire that night to stay warm,
The light from the stars guided away the storm.
It was so peaceful and quite the show,
The truth of knowledge and history I did not know.
Who had come to these mountains before us,
The conversation would turn to one of trust.
Tell no Secrets- Tell no Lies,
The sky lit up before our eyes; this must be the *"Rocky Mountain High!"*
I had never seen on vacation such a constellation,
The stars were so big there must be some correlation.
This blew my mind and I could not spend enough time,
The stars continued the light show for a very long time.
I could see Gemini, Sagittarius, and the Big Dipper,
The show was immensely gorgeous as it showed all to her.
Staying in a remote mountain cabin is the way to go,
If for nothing more than to see this great star show...

Photo by Mitchell Lao on Unsplash.com

Rollercoaster Ride

It is time to stay true to you.
You always worry about everyone else,
Now it is time, to worry about yourself.
Now it is time not to feel this way -
Take care of yourself,
So someday so can take care of me.
Someday will soon come as today.
Come over here, right away,
All I need is a hug to last all day.
Everyone needs a hug now and again,
To feel loved, wanted, encouraged in the game.
That game of life can be rough,
Just hold on and don't look down,
There is never enough ground.
It is the rollercoaster of life with its up's and downs,
You never know what's around the bend,
Not even the sound.
Don't worry I will take care of you,
As we walk down life's avenues.
This is the ride of a lifetime,
In a lifetime of rides.
If today is not good, there is always tomorrow.
Keep your mind and heart always open for a good time,
This way your heart will always be filled,
With love and rhyme for a Lifetime.

Photo by David Clarke on Unsplash.com

Running Water

Find someone you cannot live without,
Someone you cannot stop loving.
Find that special someone you cannot stop talking about,
Find a lover unlike no other to have and to hold.
It might not be about this,
It is all about that.
Maybe we should discuss this or that more,
Let us find it out now, rather than later.
We will know someday,
So forgive me for staying too long in my mind.
So bank some time with me now,
Who knows it may be worth more.
It has been said that what will come to be will be,
What will happen will happen no matter what we do,
What comes today may only happen to a few.
What comes around goes around,
Maybe it will only happen to you.
So let's run down the road,
Like the water after a rainstorm…

"THERE IS NO REMEDY FOR LOVE BUT TO LOVE MORE."
– HENRY DAVID THOREAU

Photo by Timothy Eberly on Unsplash.com

"It's one of the greatest gifts You can give yourself, To forgive."
– Maya Angelo

Seattle Nights

She gave this drifter's heart a home,
Look out Seattle; Look out LA,
I am coming home that very next day!
Look out Chicago; Look out New York,
It is raining all over the world.
We must get out before the dark of night,
Or the bright lights of the break of dawn.
Hold on for this is your song…

The park lights turn off before the morning sun,
Help me make it thru today with you.
On my own again, I am walking down the dusty road,
Nothing is ever lost, before it is owned.
Don't look at that door, when you should be wiping that floor.
I am taking these blue suede shoes down the road for you.

She gave this drifter's heart a home,
Look out Seattle; Look out LA,
I am coming home that very next day!
Look out Chicago; Look out New York,
It is raining all over the world.
We must get out before the dark of night,
Or the bright lights of the break of dawn.
Hold on for this is your song…

I can be happy anywhere with you, just you,
Any direction, even on vacation with reflection.
You are my vocation, my revelation,
There is no frustration when I'm with you.
Everything is okay, everyday,
As long as I am with you under the blue moon.
Let it shine on me, let it shine on you,
Let it shine on the whole world too.

She gave this drifter's heart a home,
Look out Seattle; Look out LA,
I am coming home that very next day!
Look out Chicago; Look out New York,
It is raining all over the world.
We must get out before the dark of night,
Or the bright lights of the break of dawn.
Hold on for this is your song…

You are all by yourself at this party looking for somebody,
You need to read the room and know the situation.
You need to read my heart there sweetheart.
Who are you calling sweetheart?
Is this only the start of romance at Midnight?
Maybe a proverbial slow dance in the celestial moonlight,
Just come over here and hold me tight.

She gave this drifter's heart a home,
Look out Seattle; Look out LA,
I am coming home that very next day!
Look out Chicago; Look out New York,
It is raining all over the world.
We must get out before the dark of night,
Or the bright lights of the break of dawn.
Hold on for this is your song…

Photo by Joel Holland on Unsplash.com

Photo by Pang Yuhao on Unsplash.com

Singapore Sings

("The Story of Yakun")

Outside the rain began and it may never end,
Cry no more to the shores of dreams.
They sail us out to sea,
For that future is thru that open door.
Forever more, forever more...
When you hear the thunder, you better take cover.
There was a lot of lightning that day,
It nearly caught me out in the bay.
Once the story is told,
It can not help but grow old.
Our ancestors left the tyranny,
To explore and to be free.
They followed their dreams once more,
Onto the shores of Singapore.
Now just follow me and you will see,
The most beautiful woman, fresh seafood, and more,
Some of the World's greatest sunsets come ashore.
We started off in the East and landed in the West,
Fire roasted our coffee and put it to the test.

We made the best kaya toast and will never look back at the rest.
Now we drift off to sleep with our head resting on Orchard Road,
Another story to be told.
My grandfather came to this place and slept on the floor near the door,
So he could hear his customer's first order in the morn.
His recipes have been preserved through all these years,
Handed down to the next generation, to his granddaughter.
Loi Ah Koon was a great man of principle, who worked hard in his restaurant,
He perfected his trade and learned a lot.
At the end of every day he would smile,
He knew his customers were comfortable and left in style.
His dreams would come true, as the restaurant grew,
He so wanted for all to enjoy his food throughout the land.
His philosophy was simple,
To work hard and enjoy what you do.
For tomorrow is but a distance in time,
Rest your weary body and close your eyes.
Everyone to this day still gathers,
Malasians, Chinese, and Filipino too,
All of us schooled in the art of family, honor, and haiku.
From here to there and everywhere,
Be grateful for all we have and all we give,
For today until all eternity lives.

"WE CANNOT BECOME
WHAT WE WANT BY
REMAINING WHAT WE ARE."
– MAX DEPREE

Photo by Mark Olsen on Unsplash.com

"Pain nourishes courage.
You can't be brave if you've
Only had wonderful things
Happen to you."
- Mary Tyler Moore

Photo by Forian Van Shreven on Unsplash.com

Sit For a While

Left bank, West bank, First bank, Go…
I'm never gonna let you go- oh, oh, oh, oh, oh.
It's cheaper than a shrink,
Come on, go get yourself a drink.
We're all grownups now,
Doing grown up things, - and how!
Let's sing about 99 beers on the wall,
I'm just sitting here with my alcohol.
Just sit back and relax,
So you don't have a heart attack, ack, ack, ack.
1. You should know by now,
All I want is a photograph and a smile.
It will last longer than that pretty -little pout,
Try harder and that smile will last for a while.
I will only stop for you, just you -
In a mile or two.
Don't relax, don't hesitate, for life is a race - somehow.

Left bank, West bank, First bank, Go...
I'm never gonna let you go - oh, oh, oh, oh, oh.
It's cheaper than a shrink,
Come on, go get yourself a drink.
We're all grownups now,
Doing grown up things, - and how!
Let's sing about 99 beers on the wall,
I'm just sitting here with my alcohol.
Just sit back and relax,
So you don't have a heart attack, ack, ack, ack.

2. All I know is how to act now that I am here,
We are here in the same place drinking alcohol,
We are one in the same, We are the same now.
Look up, It's a bird, it's a plane,
It knocks me off my chair, and wrecks my brain.
Are we all that different, or are we all the same?
We guess as if we don't know who to blame?
Is this a measure of success? Or, does it turn into future fame?

Left bank, West bank, First bank, Go...
I'm never gonna let you go - oh, oh, oh, oh, oh.
It's cheaper than a shrink,
Come on, go get yourself a drink.
We're all grownups now,
Doing grown up things- and how!
Let's sing about 99 beers on the wall,
I'm just sitting here with my alcohol.
Just sit back and relax,
So you don't have a heart attack, ack, ack, ack.

3. Who are you?

Come sit with me; come drink with me,

Come dance with me, romance with me.

I have a hankering this won't last all night,

You are quit the sight, sitting in that dim lit room,

Sitting there on a pretend honeymoon,

Will that image end too soon?

Maybe we should get a Room.

Left bank, West bank, First bank, Go...

I'm never gonna let you go - oh, oh, oh, oh, oh.

It's cheaper than a shrink,

Come on, go get yourself a drink.

We're all grownups now,

Doing grown up things- and how!

Let's sing about 99 beers on the wall,

I'm just sitting here with my alcohol.

Just sit back and relax,

So you don't have a heart attack, ack, ack, ack.

4. Am I Alowishus, Aristotle, or Ulysses?

Let us run to that corner or we will miss it.

Maybe, I'm not the one you long for,

Maybe a forlorn attempt to escape all together.

Is real life not what you were meant for,

Is that some fantasy that makes you run for the door.

Do you ignore or not listen at all,

Why not just listen and stop spending all that time away.

That is all I have to say...

Left bank, West bank, First bank, Go...
I'm never gonna let you go - oh, oh, oh, oh, oh.
It's cheaper than a shrink,
Come on, go get yourself a drink.
We're all grownups now,
Doing grown up things- and how!
Let's sing about 99 beers on the wall,
I'm just sitting here with my alcohol.
Just sit back and relax,
So you don't have a heart attack, ack, ack, ack.

Photo by Johannes Plenio on Unsplash.com

"All our dreams can come True if we have the Courage to pursue them." -Walt Disney

"Be so good they can't ignore you."

-Steve Martin

Photo by Alexandr Podvain on Unsplash.com

Summertime

Grab a glass of wine, it's Summertime.
I want a shot of tequila with you,
Spending a little time with you,
Under that old oak tree.
You know I can't love you that way anymore,
You love me more, than I can anymore.
We lay in the sun and lather up, so we don't burn,
When you touch me that way it makes me laugh and squirm.
Let's go jump in the lake and swim for a while,
You drive me wild for miles and miles.
Just getting back on track is hard,
We are moving and not looking back; it's a start.
I need you a little more each night,
Do you know I love you and will get it right?
Let's go back to beach and swim under the moonlight.
Sippin' on whiskey after the barbeque,
Just sittin' here thinking of you.
It is my favorite time of year,
It is Summertime here.

Photo by Kenta Kikuchi on Unsplash.com

SUMMER

Summer is about zip lines, fishing lines, and good times.
Roller coasters, hikes with strollers, and ice cream posers.
Summer is for outdoor parks, motorcycle rides, and pool slides.
Laying in the sun, reading for fun, and hanging out until we are done.
Road trips, beer sips, cow tips, and trampoline flips.
Looking for friends, playing pretend, staying up until ten,
And seeing fireflies spend.
Summer is staying with family on the lake, barbecuing at eight,
And trying to keep it straight.
Watching baseball games, eating hot dogs, and staying up until dawn.
Swimming, diving, a little conniving, with plenty of time for surprising.
Ups and downs, all around town, clowning around without a sound.
Summer is about playing games, holding hands, seeing bands,
And planting herbs in the ground.
Watching children playing, masquerading, enjoying every minute,
Of every day until the sun fades away…

Photo by Hester Qiang on Unsplash.com

THAT IS ALL I KNOW (so far)

Make every day count as your last,
Always look forward and learn from your past.
Do not put off until tomorrow, what you can do today.
Do unto others as you would want done unto you,
That is the "golden rule" and my last name too.
Always measure twice and cut once,
Tell your family you Love them every day, once or twice.
Never run on empty or you will run out of gas,
Write every day to make it last…
Listen to your body and get plenty of rest.
Never guess someone's weight or age,
Always be kind and get used to change.
Look both ways before you cross the street,
Always count and check your Halloween candy,
Make sure there are less tricks than treats.
Never count one's chickens before they hatch,
Always choose the right path, Man plans and God laughs…
Never run with a knife or scissors in your hand,
You can never have too many friends.
A smile is a free way to brighten someone's day,
Laughing is better than crying anytime.
Never hold it inside, try to keep it off your mind.
Patience is a learned skill that you have to practice,
Every ten years treat yourself to a new mattress.
You can never have too many memories or pictures,
Winning is not important, working together is…
Aim for your dreams, but do not lose yourself along the way.
Teamwork makes the Dream work. Happy wife, happy Life…

Photo by Connor Bowe on Unsplash.com

The RIGHT Way

If you are thinking what I am thinking...
This is the mark in a moment in time,
A mark turning an entire nation of minds.
Pulling the trigger on right from wrong,
Causing this writer to take a pause.

Is the right way of the past, the right way that will last?
Is it a matter of circumstance in an impossible fray?
It is only a matter of time, where no Mankind, will know what to say.

In that little lead way we know of today,
Who is to say what is right in the right way.
Who is to continue This line of questioning in the same way?
Remove yourself from the insanity, the selfishness, the nonsense of it all.
Begin to heal this plight, this flight, this fall...

Photo by Morgan David on Unsplash.com

Istock Photo on Unsplash.com

The Rules of Golf

(According to Will Reuhl)

1. You do not need to be good; you just don't want to be slow (play at a steady pace).

2. Enjoy the Day (Carpe Diem-If you love the outdoors, you will love golf)!

3. Try to stay relaxed - do not over think the game (do not get in your own way).

4. Keep your Head down (lifting your head lifts your club and will give you a bad shot).

5. Pretend it is just you and the ball (you are not competing against anyone but yourself (and the course).

6. Do Not Bet on Golf, betting money creates undo pressure (if you want to give away your money, donate it to a children's charity).

7. If you hit a bad shot, "Laugh it off" (sometimes golf like life, hands you lemons-make Lemonade)!

8. Be humble and courteous (always yield to your fellow golfers - No road rage allowed).

9. Be Careful and Safe (do not walk ahead or stand in front when someone is hitting a golf ball).

10. Never give advice or lessons on the golf course (the exception is only if someone asks for help).

"SUCCESS ALWAYS DEMANDS A GREATER EFFORT."
- WINSTON CHURCHILL

Photo by Jorge Franco on Unsplash.com

"Only if we understand can we care. Only if we care will we help."
-Jane Goodall

The Significance of Twelve (12)

If you are born on the 12th of March, a Pisces you will be!

Pisces is the twelfth astrological sign, out of twelve zodiac signs to see.

A dozen donuts, a dozen eggs, a dozen cycles of the moon,

Twelve people have walked on the moon; is that too much, or too soon?

"That's one step for man. One giant leap for mankind." –Neil Armstrong

One foot is a dozen inches. Soon to finish, too soon to be done,

A dozen roses for the perfect one.

Time, measured in two increments of twelve.

Twelve o'clock is Noon or Midnight. A.m. or p.m. will do.

We will meet at high noon in the middle of town for an old Western shootout.

Was this a showdown in old town by Wild Bill and Dave Tutt? Shut up...

Before the clock strikes midnight, Cinderella...

"Where will you go when the clock strikes twelve?

What will you do when you face yourself?

How will you live knowing what you have done?

How will you die if your soul's already gone?"

– Excerpt of monologue from Compasia & Eratosthenes, as performed by Willem Denbury - book by Marie Lu, *The Midnight Star* (The Young Elites #3) published in 2016.

If a clock is stuck on twelve, will it be correct twice a day?

Twelve days of Christmas, a partridge in a pear tree. Is this of significance to thee?

The Twelfth Hour - one of twelve equal or nearly equal parts of an object, quantity, or measure.

January 6 is the twelfth day after Christmas and the feast of the Epiphany forever.

The Twelfth man refers to the fans in the stands at a football game.

The evening of the Twelfth day. The eve of the twelfth day or the evening of January 5.

The number twelve carries religious, mythological and magical symbolism, generally representing perfection. (These are all facts of 12, according to Wikipedia).

Twelve is a symbol of cosmic order.

Twelve is the number of space and time.

Twelve is my lucky number and blows my mind.

This was twelve times harder to write than just one line.

There are twelve months of the year. Not just the third month, I fear.

The twelfth card of Tarot is the card of the hanged man and is symbolic of self-sacrifice and meditation.

The Flag of the European Union has twelve stars.

There are usually twelve people on a jury (a jury of our peers).

Twelve Sage Leaves (used to find ones spouse in April).

The twelve Tribes of Israel. (Jacob had twelve sons. Do you remember Joseph?)

The twelve Apostles of Jesus: Peter, Andrew, James, John, Philip, Bartholomew, Matthew, Thomas, James the Less, Simon the Zealot, Thaddeus, and Judas Iscariot.

Twelve Pillars - Twelve Tribes. Was this a surprise or a Biblical- reprise.

I work twelve hours a day, sometimes twelve days in a row...

The Hawaiian alphabet has twelve letters, of this I know.

Magnesium has the Atomic number twelve.

Twelve Grapes for Good Luck - eat twelve grapes at the stroke of midnight on New Year's Eve for good luck the next year! (as you eat, count one grape for each month)

The Twelve Olympians refers to the 12 principle gods that resided on Mount Olympus: Zeus, Hera, Poseidon, Ares, Hermes, Hephaistos, Aphrodite, Athena, Apollo, Artimis, Demeter, and Hestia.

The Twelve Labours of Heracles - impossible tasks that he completed, according to Greek mythology.

"The number twelve is the result of 4x3, four elements, four corners of the earth, four cardinal points. When these are multiplied 4x3, three being the sacred number of God, the result is twelve - the perfect number"- a significance of twelve also found in Wikipedia.

There was a twelve- minute delay on the I-12 today, which caused a twelve-car pileup in May.

That last rhyme has no significance to the number twelve, which is fine, says the number nine.

"The first wealth
is health."
- Ralph Waldo Emerson

"Living in the past is ego, Living in the future pride, Living in the present is humility."
-Giannis Antetokounmpo, Milwaukee Bucks Champion 2021

Photo by Jeremy Bishop on Unsplash.com

Three Seconds (in a lifetime...)

Three seconds, three minutes, three hours, three times faster,
Is three better than one? Let us look a little closer.
Are you three times better if you arrive three minutes early?
Would not nine be three times better to be?
What about twenty-one? Are you an adult at twenty-one?
Is that seven times better to me...
Has that determined how long you live?
It means you will be twenty-one three more times!
Is the average life expectancy now eighty-four?
What about the Golden years of sixty?
Are we twenty times wiser than we were at three?
How long does it take to realize what could be?
Will I be able to climb a tree at sixty-three?
Can I swim the Ocean blue at Ninety-two?
What if I live to be one hundred three?
Are you now three times more likely to be struck by lightning,
Than to win the lottery?
Was Einstein really Thirty-three when he discovered Relativity?
Is it good luck if it comes in threes?
Then, why do celebrities die in threes?
Do you want to three-peat, make a three pointer, or kick a field goal?
Is it a good thing to let your phone ring three times?
What about going to your favorite spot three times and stay three times longer?
Do you let a doorbell ring three times before you answer the door?
How do you know if you are three times smarter when you hit the floor?
Who is keeping score?
I just wish to fall asleep three times faster, before I snore...

Photo by Jose Martinez on Unsplash.com

"Nobody has ever measured,
not even poets, how much
the heart can hold."
-Zelda Fitzgerald

Together Forever?

When we stay together in any kind of weather,
We settle down with each other forever.
The boat will rock back and forth with rhythm,
Like my favorite song on the radio by Him.
We pray that this night will never end,
We send a letter in a bottle and pretend.
Someone, someday will find out love is real,
Like time in a bottle or those who will follow...
So lay back and relax; Let us make a deal for contrast.
Maybe, just maybe we are the last ones on this planet,
Go ahead and throw a party, and make it a habit.
Invite everyone we know, even Uncle Joe.
This could be the door to nowhere,
Maybe a door to somewhere...
No matter what- Are we heading the wrong way?
We have to say, this could be our last day.
So grab me now, or grab me then and again,
I just want the chance to see you again in heaven.
Tell everyone you know that I am your friend,
You should already know -
It is up to you to stay until the end...

Photo by Ivana Cajina on Unsplash.com

Too Much

Too much rain,

Too much pain.

Too much rage,

Too much fade.

Too much sun,

Too much fun.

Too much riding,

Too much confining.

Too much money,

Too much honey.

Too much stress,

Too much mess.

Too much sleep,

Too much weep.

Too much noise,

Too much toys.

Too much waste,

Too much in your face.

"The only difference between success and failure is the ability to take action."
– Alexander Graham Bell

Photo by Ruffa Jane Reyes on Unsplash.com

"Freedom consists not in doing what we like, But in having the right to do what we ought."
-Pope John Paul II

UP

Wake up, pull up, sneak up, speak up, walk up, move up,
Eat up, fold up, sun - up, hurry up, sit up, look up.
Be up, sum up, sign up, last up, free up, always up,
Lay - up, close - up, never up, early up, laid up, curtains up.
You're up (Europe), way up, toss up, heads up, sup,
Tied up, once up, one up, two up, three up, four...
Conjure up, break up, dress up, lift - up, go up, What's up,
Push up, save up, live it up, seize up, back up, buy up.
Huddle up, settle - up, shut up, turn up (turnip), sound up,
Zipper up, round up, listen up, hands up, rise - up, fire up.
Lock up, ride up, windows up, trays up, flaps up, hurry up,
Climb up, reach up, thumbs up, make up, start up, way up,
Write up, mess up, sit up, step up, rile up, sweep up,
Trade up, right up, everybody up, cuddle up, freeze up.
Time is up.

Photo by Farida Davletshin on Unsplash.com

Walk on the Beach

Walking on the beach with the sand between my toes,
Moving swiftly, but not too fast or slow.
Taking in the sun, sea, and sand,
With moved from one Tiki bar to the next with no plans.
Starting at the Sunset Grill - Oh what a thrill!
Ending at the JW beachcomber bar was the best so far.
From the jelly fish in the lobby to bowling in the tower,
We could have spent more time people watching and smelling flowers.
Next was the Snook Inn for seafood during the dinner hour.
Marco Island had everything to offer: clear waters, gorgeous homes,
Great restaurants to help you feel at home.
There were yachts, fishing boats, and sailboats too,
So much on the Island, we did not know what to do.
We admired and dreamed of the yachts in the harbor,
It made us begin to wonder...
What would happen if we went out to sea,
On a Yacht with one, two, or three.
To sleep below deck or cook in the galley,
Sun bathe on the upper deck or race in a rally.
Get me a captain's hat and maybe an ascot,
We are ready to depart and I want to look the part.
White sand beaches do not get hot in the sun,
Marco and Naples are certainly a lot of fun.
There were more shells at Barefoot Beach then I had ever seen,
We collected them all day as a grandparent collecting machine.
It really felt like a dream; I was the captain of that team.
The ocean was too cold, so we played cards, read, and slept on the beach,
A great way to end a vacation with good friends, good weather, and good cheer.

Photo by Neonbrand Lod on Unsplash.com

Warm Hugs

A hug means I need you,
A hug means you really care.
A hug is worth a million,
A hug comes with a spare.
A hug is like taking a walk on a warm summer night,
A hug is an electric blanket, a personal delight.
A hug is like being tucked-in at night,
A hug is a security blanket to a young child,
A hug gives strength, courage, and might.
A hug is a special moment, that place, that time,
A hug keeps you going for miles and miles ahead.
A hug puts a smile on your face,
A hug reminds you of that special place.
A hug makes us all human, wanted, needed, and more,
A hug makes it easier to get thru a hard day.
A hug is to show someone you care,
A hug is a long shot against the fray.
A hug should be given more than it is received,
A hug could be a part of the birds and bees.
A hug makes the World a better place for all to share,
A hug in every way shows everyone that you really care.
A hug, even virtual, will be from you to me and me to you,
Forever More...

Photo by Phillip Pils on Unsplash.com

Where Eagles Soar

I climbed to the top of the mountain to see what I would see,
All I saw was an eagle standing in his nest looking at me.
The eagle asked, "Why are you here?"
I replied, "To learn to soar above it all, no matter how near or far."
"Just spread your wings out and follow me," said the Eagle.
I began to swoop and float and flutter. It was very surreal…
It began to be overwhelming, fearful, and tall,
My strength seemed to wander, and I began to fall.
The eagle said, "Clear your mind and let the natural currents take you away!"
I thanked the eagle and flew away into the stratosphere that sunny day.
Learning an enormous lesson to set my sights on the horizon and not the hill,
Be blind to the future and never settle for man's will.
For man plans and God laughs.
Always be open to adventure and what is in plain sight.
Concentrate on the present, learn from the past, and look forward to the future!
We can always learn from nature, our children, and our spiritual rest,
Control what you can control and always do your Best…

"Don't put off until tomorrow what you can do today." - Benjamin Franklin

Photo by Dylan Taylor on Unsplash.com

Where the Wildflowers Grow

Take me to the mountains where the wildflowers grow,
Take me down to Mexico or maybe even Colorado!
Where the monarch butterflies fly free,
Where they migrate, mate, and fly among the trees.
Springtime brings the wildflowers bloom and color on the ground,
With bright yellows, purples, blues, oranges, and brown.
As far as the eyes can see, there is foliage all around.
The trees, the flowers, and the bees are all you seek,
Into the mountains again with a rise and a peak.
We conquer the summit, Buffalo Peak and even see snow,
Just a gentle breeze, a deep breath at ten thousand feet - Here we go.
It is called, high country paradise, South Park, a map to follow,
A prairie like flat land that spans across tomorrow.
The sun finally came out that first day around ten,
We took the morning to check out downtown with friends.
There was hiking, kayaking, whitewater rafting, and even mountain biking,
A town built on a river, the perfect day, how exciting!
We saw mule deer, elk, and even some buffalo,
The temperature started to drop; it might even snow!
Mountains filled with clean air and sunshine,
Always smart to hike in pairs to stay fine.
The stars came out at night and put on a show for free,
The sky was so bright it even illuminated me.
A mountain is a wonderful quiet escape,
Getting back to nature is a piece of cake.
Ask me once, ask me twice, I don't know,
Being in touch with nature is the way to go...

Photo by Jackson Simmer on Unsplash.com

Photo by That's her Business- on Unsplash.com

Words from Confusion

We need to take advantage of the weather when the weather is good.
I do not know where I am going, but I will know when I get there.
It is easier to thread a needle, than stopping a charging buffalo.
It is easier to compromise, than argue about nothing.
Look at the world thru the eyes of a child, then everyone will be your friend.
Do not spit in the wind, unless you want to get wet!
The world is full of miracles, go out and make one.
Your glass is always half full, not half-empty.
You have a chance of a lifetime in a lifetime of chances.

Photo by Ryan Riggins on Unsplash.com

Words of Wisdom

Too heavy, too fast, this will not last!

Too light, too slow, it just won't show, look both ways before you go.

You need to pass thru, cartoon, see it thru, help your fellow man or foe.

You need to pass the buck, see the puck, build your luck, get out of the muck.

Nothing is ever accomplished when you do it half way, Nothing ventured, nothing gained.

Nothing ever lasts, just ask the right way, today, on plane, on a train?

That is water under the bridge, something to save for a rainy day.

That is a message in a bottle, a new day, something you should not say.

A penny earned is a penny saved, Do not spend it all in the same place.

A wise man once said, face your fears head on - stay up until the break of dawn.

Do as I say not as I do, the rest is up to you, Do unto others as you would have done unto you!

Do it right the first time or do not do it at all, measure twice and cut once, Just do it!

Don't put off to tomorrow what you can do today, I have a dream, what will be will be?

Don't spit into the wind, Don't bite the hand that feeds you, Don't close your mind to the possibilities.

Wish on that star, No matter who you are, Wash away today for a brand new day.

Wish for a better tomorrow, make a wish it may come true, wishing wells made for you.

Water under the bridge, Let it roll off your back, rub dirt on it, and it will never come back.

Water it and it will grow, read it and you will know, climb every mountain, and conquer all your fears.

Ultimate power corrupts ultimately, think out of the box, plan your work, and work your plan.

Ultimately, we all get to the same place, the end does not justify the means, Do what you Love.

Never look back, don't step on a crack, don't break a mirror, don't stand here.

Never look directly in the sun, always do your best and have fun, always walk, never run.

Don't sweat the small stuff and it is all small stuff, control what you can control.

Don't put off until tomorrow what you can do today, you can only control yourself.

Do it yourself, try-try- try again, you will never know what you can do until you try.

Do what you want, want what you may, you may get burned, so don't play with fire...

Photo by Michal Parzucho on Unsplash.com

You Come as You Are

Believe in what you see,
He is a mystery.
Praise him, Oh Praise him now.
The Lord is the only one,
He is my salvation...

From day to day, I may go astray,

He is my destiny.
My luck continues to build thru the light,
He has come to show the way, the truth, and the life.

Believe in what you see,
He is a mystery.
Praise him, Oh Praise him now.
The Lord is the only one,
He is my salvation...

Follow me, you shall be redeemed,
More abundant, free, and pristine.
A window where you will see me,
It will clear, justified, and next to the tree.

Believe in what you see,
He is a mystery.
Praise him, Oh, Praise him now.
The Lord is the only one,
He is my salvation...
Am I a part of your kingdom, your family, your majesty?
Your river and cup will run dry without me.
Lift your prayer forever to me,
What will be, will be...

Believe in what you see,
He is a mystery.
Praise him, Oh, Praise him now.
The Lord is the only one,
He is my salvation...

I was lost but now am found, blind but now see,
You called out my name and stood by my side.
Come as you are and hear my call,
I am the Lord of all.

Believe in what you see,
He is a mystery.
Praise him, Oh, Praise him now.
The Lord is the only one,
He is my salvation...

Photo by Shaojie on Unsplash.com

"The most important thing in communication is hearing what isn't said."

- Peter F. Drucker

Istock photo on Unsplash.com